Rapid Problem-Solving
with
Post-it® Notes

For Eleri

While Honey lies in Every Flower, no doubt,
It takes a Bee to get the Honey out.

Arthur Guiterman, *A Poet's Proverbs*, 1924

Rapid Problem-Solving with Post-it® Notes

David Straker

Gower

Published by
Gower Publishing Limited
Gower House
Croft Road
Aldershot
Hampshire GU11 3HR
England

Gower
Old Post Road
Brookfield
Vermont 05036
USA

David Straker has asserted his right under the Copyright, Designs and Patents Act 1988 to be identified as the author of this work.

British Library Cataloguing in Publication Data
Straker, David
    Rapid Problem solving with Post-it Notes
    1. Problem solving 2. Problem solving - Equipment and supplies
    I. Title
    153.4'3

ISBN 0 566 07836 8

        Library of Congress Cataloging-in-Publication Data

Straker, David.
    Rapid problem solving with Post-it Notes / David Straker.
    p.   cm.
    ISBN 0-566-07836-8 (cloth)
    1. Sticky notes. 2. Paperwork (Office practice) - -Management.
    I. Title.
    HF5547. 15.S77 1996
    651.7'4- -dc20   96-28070
                                                        CIP

Typeset in Times New Roman, Arial and Lucida Handwriting by David Straker and printed in Great Britain by Hartnolls Limited, Bodmin.

Contents

Acknowledgements

Books are seldom written by a single person in isolation, and this one is no exception. I have had much help from many friends and family along the way, so this is a big thank you to at least:

At HP:– for encouragement and suggestions, Peter Auber, Simon Bedford-Roberts, David Gee, John Hamilton, Philip Nield, Doug O'Hanlon and David Whittall.

At 3M:– Carolyn Morris, for support and supplies, plus Spence Silver, Art Fry, and others for the original glue, idea and development of the magical Post-it® Note.

At Gower:– Malcolm Stern and Solveig Servian for faith and everything that publishers do.

At his place:– Simon Kitson for the splendid cartoons.

At home:– Eleri, Heledd, Geraint and Bella for love, patience and much, much more.

And not forgetting:– You, for buying the book, plus everyone else who lent a hand, an ear, a thought or other support during writing, review and production. Thank you.

Introduction

Do you ever come across problems which seem to be a morass of issues, disagreement and disconnected pieces of information? Do you go around in circles for hours or days, arguing and trying to make sense of it all? If so, you are in good company–many other people face such problems every day. It is a sad fact of the messy world in which we must live and work that problems don't come in tidy packages that are easy to understand and solve.

So what is the answer? It is that problems are almost invariably made up of discrete pieces of information which are related to each other in some way. The size of the problem is simply determined by a combination of the number of information pieces and the number and type of relationships *between* these pieces. Whether your problem is to build a house, to analyse competitive positioning or to plan a meal, all you need to know is what the pieces are and how they may be organized to help you understand the problem and produce an effective solution.

Never fear–help is at hand! Armed with this book and a pad of Post-it® Notes, you can bring order to the chaos, coaxing the pieces of your jigsaw puzzle into place.

How can Post-it® Notes help?

Post-it® Notes have three key properties that we can use to help solve these difficult problems:

- Firstly, they are about the right size to hold one piece of information from a problem.
- Secondly, they are easy to attach to a smooth surface and stay where they are put.
- Thirdly, they can be quickly and easily detached and reattached many times.

These properties make Post-it® Notes an ideal basic tool for use in rapid problem-solving. The missing factor, however, is the method. *How* do you get all the right pieces of information, and *how* do you organize them to help solve your problem?

That is where this book comes in. It describes a set of tools that are quick and easy to learn and use, allowing you to get to the heart of your problem rapidly and easily. Complex tools are fine for specialists, but most working people have neither the time nor the energy to delve into the details of sophisticated analytical techniques.

Simple names are used for simple tools. Impressive sounding names may add to the mystique of specialists, but can be off-putting for other people.

Finally, the tools are described clearly and practically, with many diagrams and examples. The aim, after all, is for you to *use* them, not just be impressed or understand the theory.

3M and Post-it® Notes

In 1968, Spence Silver, a chemist at 3M, was developing adhesives, when he came up with a weak 'unsticky' adhesive. There were many attempts to find a use for it in a product. Eventually, an associate called Art Fry, who was also an enthusiastic choir director, discovered a use for the adhesive. One day in 1974, after the bookmarks fell out of his hymnal, he thought about Silver's adhesive. The result was the now-famous Post-it® Notes.

Post-it® Notes did not become successful immediately—in fact they only took off after a concerted campaign, culminating in 1978 with a significant market give-away promotion, where a large proportion of the people who received the free samples proved the value of the product by coming back for more.

3M own the brand-name 'Post-it®' and ask that each and every time it is used, the symbol for a registered trade-mark, ®, is put alongside it. They also note that 'Post-it' is an adjective and must be used as such, as there are a whole range of other Post-it® products.

Although the book may look a little like it was written by or for 3M, this is not so. Post-it® Notes are a serious business tool that can be used for rapid problem-solving. Because the registered trade-mark symbol sprinkled throughout a book can detract from its readability, the word 'Note' (spot the initial capital) has been freely used instead. Thus, where you see the word 'Note', please read Post-it® Note.

Tool origins

Most tools are based on previous learning, and the Post-it® Note tools described in this book are no different. To a greater or lesser degree, they have been borrowed and adapted from existing methods of solving problems (see table).

Tool	Origins
Post-up	Brainstorming, Brainwriting, Nominal Group Technique, Crawford Slip Method
Swap Sort	Bubble Sort, Paired Comparison, Prioritization Matrix
Top-down Tree	Systematic/Tree Diagram, Cause–Effect Diagram, Why–Why Diagram, How–How Diagram, Process Decision Program Chart
Bottom-up Tree	Affinity Diagram, KJ Method, Set theory
Information Map	Interrelationship Digraph/Relations Diagram, Mind Map, Entity–Relation Diagram, State-Transition Diagram
Action Map	Activity Network, PERT Diagram, Process Flowchart, Data Flow Diagram

And finally...

Only you can make these tools work. If you think this is a great book and put it on the shelf without using the tools it describes to solve your problems, it will have failed. If, however, you use one tool to help solve one problem, then it will have begun to succeed.

A Quick Tour

Are you impatient to get going? Are you browsing and just want to find out what rapid problem-solving with Post-it® Notes means? Do you use the tools already and just want a quick reminder? If the answer to any of these questions is 'yes', then this section is for you.

If you want to start with the background information, about how the tools work and the basic details of using them, then go to Part I. This section is for people in a hurry who want to see the big picture first, then the detailed bits later.

A Quick Tour

Key principles

Rapid problem solving with Post-it® Notes uses a few key principles to help you understand your problems and find the important decision points. Here is a quick summary of those key principles–enough to start you off, but not so much as to slow you down on your hurricane tour.

Chunking

- Your mind works by taking in information one discrete piece, or *chunk*, at a time – be it a simple chunk like 'a brick', or a more complex chunk, such as 'my house'.
- Information on problems also come in chunks. It can usually be written in a short phrase or sentence, for example, 'The roof is leaking'.
- You can capture problem chunks by writing them on Notes.
- You can solve problems by:
  – finding all the chunks
  – arranging them into meaningful patterns
  – homing in on the important bits.

Problem patterns

There are three basic ways of arranging chunks:

- *Lists* are simple collections of chunks which may or may not be sorted into an order of importance.
- *Trees* have simple hierarchical 'parent and child' relationships. They can be built top-down or bottom-up.
- *Maps* have more complex relationships, with any chunk related to any other chunk. They can be used to relate specific actions or more general information chunks.

Guiding decisions

- Simple written guidelines help keep sessions on track.
- *Objectives* describe what you are trying to achieve. Non-objectives make clear what you are *not* trying to achieve.
- *Criteria* are the judgement points for making decisions, for example, 'must be low cost'.
- *Questions* stimulate and direct thinking.
- *Constraints* limit your choices, for example, 'Only John and Jean can use the PR30'.

The FOG factor

- An information chunk can be a fact, an opinion or a guess.
- *Facts* can be proved to be true. They are usually more useful, but are also harder to find or prove.
- *Opinions* are what people believe to be true. They are often mistaken for facts.
- *Guesses* are acknowledged as wild ideas.
- You can write F, O or G on a Note to indicate whether the chunk is a fact, opinion or guess.
- It is often worth taking time to find information that will change important opinions or guesses into known facts.

Note sessions

- The Post-it® Note tools can be used on your own, but are more often used in meetings with other people who can contribute to solving the problem.
- The guidelines for each tool can be displayed on a separate flipchart, where everyone can see them.

The Post-up

- The Post-up is the first List tool.
- Use it for collecting information chunks, one per Note.
- In a group, everyone writes chunks and sticks them up at the same time. They do not talk whilst they are doing this. The result is a focused and efficient information collection session.

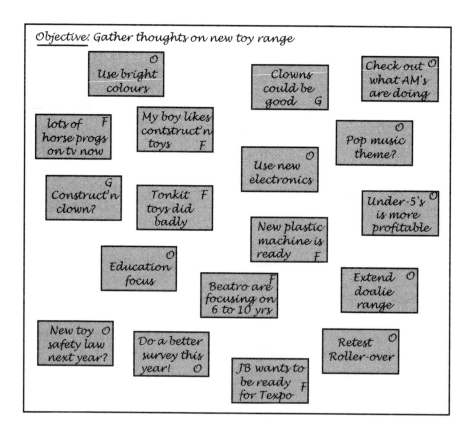

The Swap Sort

- The Swap Sort is the second List tool.
- Use it to sort chunks into an order of importance.
- First reduce the list is by combining similar items and rejecting low priority ones.
- Sort by swapping pairs of Notes, putting the most important one higher up in the list, until no more can be swapped.
- Use the same criterion in each comparison to find the most important Note of each pair.

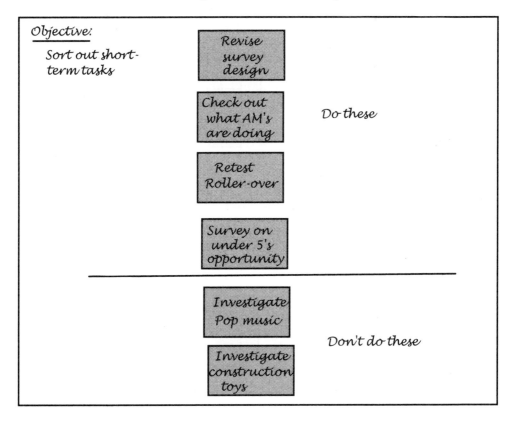

The Top-down Tree

- The Top-down Tree is the first Tree tool.
- Use it to break down a problem when you have little existing information.
- Do this by asking a consistent question of each Note.

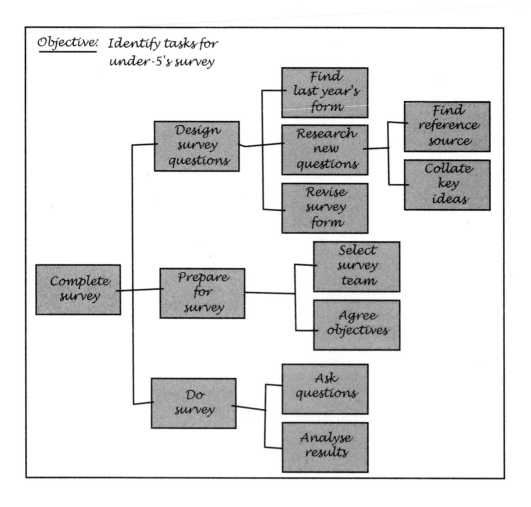

The Bottom-up Tree

- The Bottom-up Tree is the second Tree tool.
- Use it when you have lots of information chunks, but do not understand the fundamental nature of the problem.
- Build up the tree by forming groups of Notes, then grouping the groups and so on until there is one 'top-level' group.
- Give each group a title to describe what it contains.

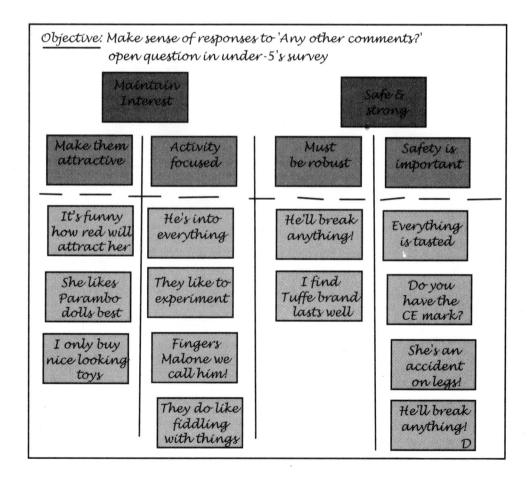

The Information Map

- The Information Map is the first Map tool.
- Use it to map messy problems, where information chunks have complex interrelationships.
- First identify chunks and place related ones near one another, then show the relationships with arrows.

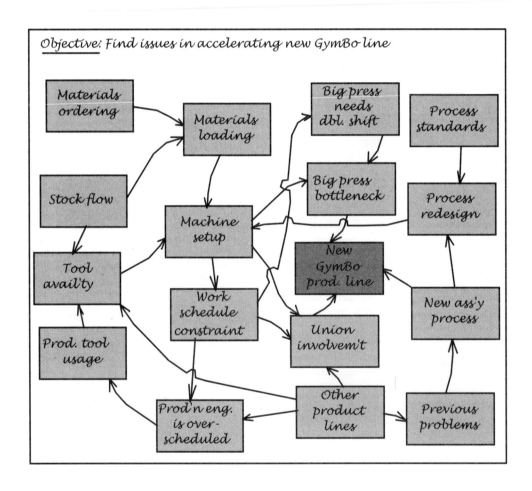

The Action Map

- The Action Map is the second Map tool.
- Use it to plan actions or to map an existing process.
- Use one chunk for each action, then place them in order of action.
- Add arrows to show this order more clearly.

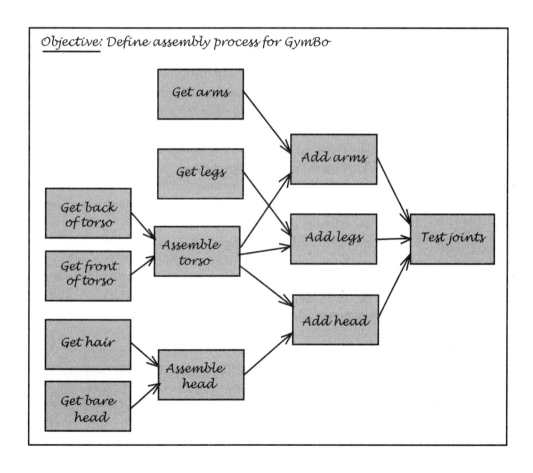

Tools in Practice

The Post-it® Note tools are of little value unless you make practical use of them.

Frameworks

You can make the process of solving problems more predictable and reliable by using a *framework*–a simple and flexible set of guidelines to help you structure your approach. The complexity of the method should match the importance and complexity of your problem.

- *Questioning approach*–use basic questions to help probe the problem and find an appropriate solution.
- *Simple framework*–use three simple steps to help you solve your problem:
    1. What are you trying to achieve?
    2. Where is the *real* problem?
    3. What is the solution?
- *Project framework*–use six, more detailed steps:
    1. What is the problem?
    2. Why is it happening?
    3. How can I fix it?
    4. Fix it!
    5. Why did it work or not work?
    6. What next?

Extended use

Once you have mastered the tools, you can become more creative about where and how they are used.

By combining discipline and experimentation you can find out what works best for you.

Part I

How the Post-it® Note Tools Work

It is one thing to have a set of tools, it is another to make them work well. So before you begin using the Post-it® Note tools for solving your difficult problems, pause a while and read Part I. It is intended to stop you from falling into some common problem-solving traps and to make the tools work well for you.

Using Post-it® Notes?

1 Understanding Problems

Problems come in all shapes and sizes, but many have common characteristics that can be addressed with the Post-it® Note tools described in Part II of this book. You may be launching a new advertising campaign, investigating production line rejects or planning a dinner-party, but each situation contains pieces of information that can be found and organized, making solving the problem both easier and more enjoyable.

This chapter describes these pieces of information, how to find them and fit them together in patterns so that you can make effective decisions that help to solve those difficult problems.

Sales are falling

I wish it were summer

Customers are complaining

My salary has not gone up this year

The Cossor keeps breaking down

Jim looks unwell

Oil prices are rising

Jane is pregnant

Memory chips are scarce

Sarah likes Mike

The weather is fine

Red and black look nice together

Business is booming

6mm screws weigh 23g

RamCo looks like a good buy

Pieces of information
(Is this everything? What do they all <u>mean</u>?)

Chunks

The connection between problems and the way we understand them can be described in one word–chunks.

What is a chunk?

The human mind is continuously being battered with vast amounts of information–so how do we cope with it? The answer is that we divide it into digestible chunks. Thus, when you look out of the window, instead of seeing a mass of shapes and hues, you recognize a tree, a road or a car. Each of these is a 'chunk' that your mind can interpret as a single item.

Problems and information can similarly be recognized in distinct chunks. We describe each chunk in a brief statement or phrase, such as 'capture imagination of young people', 'casing often fractures' or 'provide smooth flow of entertainment'.

We can deal with a problem by recognizing and organizing its component chunks in ways that reveal new and interesting information chunks that help us to make decisions and identify the important actions which will solve the problem.

Using the Post-it® Note tools described in this book we write one chunk on each Note. The Notes' unique ability to be detached and re-attached enables us to move them around to form meaningful structures and relationships.

This book is written in chunks too. Each topic forms a single visual chunk which is aimed at helping you to understand it in one go, without having to page back and forth.

What makes a good chunk?

Each Note contains a single chunk of information that is easy to read and understand.

Chunks of information on Notes often have a basic verb–noun or adjective–noun structure, as they say what is happening to what:

> e.g. 'Broken fixture' or 'Unhappy customer'.

Other information may be added that helps describe the situation, but the whole chunk must still be clear and concise.

> e.g. 'Broken fixture on bath' or 'Customer unhappy about delays'.

A good example:
> 'Many customer complaints about service delays.'

Not so good examples:
> 'Many complaints.'

> 'There have been quite a few telephone calls from people who
> have complained long and loud about the time it takes to
> get some attention so that their problem can be attended to.'

Finding and choosing chunks

Two common situations may arise when you are problem-solving. Either you may have too little information or you may have plenty of information, but can make little sense of it. In the first situation, the initial task must be to find the information chunks that will help you solve the problem. In the latter situation, you may want to find the important pieces that will require further attention.

Finding chunks

When you are looking for information chunks, be they problems, causes or solutions, there is a common tendency to identify only the obvious. Many people, for example, will jump rapidly to what they believe is the one good solution. This is wrong. There are usually many good solutions and the key to finding the best solution is first to find a number of good alternatives.

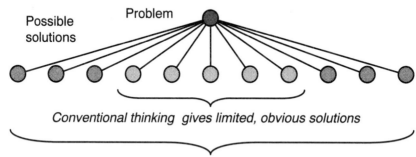

Divergence in problem-solving

This *divergent* approach will help you to find more information chunks than with 'conventional' thinking. To be successful at divergent thinking you must break down the habitual thinking patterns that most people use to make their lives easier to understand and control.

Post-it® Note tools can help with divergence. The Post-up is particularly good for *creative* divergence, where you are looking for new and original ideas. The Top-down Tree is good for *logical* divergence, where you are breaking down a problem into its constituent parts. Maps can help stimulate relational divergence (which may be logical or creative).

Who make good divergent thinkers?

- Children, who have not yet been coerced into conventional thinking.
- Comedians, who find unexpected fun in commonplace situations.
- International negotiators, who find agreeable solutions to intractable differences.

You, when you set your mind free.

Choosing chunks

Divergence will help you to identify many chunks, but the problem then is to make sense of it all and to select specific chunks on which to act. This transition from having many chunks to a few (often just one) is called *convergence*.

A divergent activity is almost always followed by convergent activity, sorting the wheat from the chaff, selecting those items that are to be carried forward for further action. A long, multistage problem-solving process can be kept manageable by using divergence and convergence at each stage to find and carry forward the best alternative.

One danger of convergence is that people may become too conservative, with the result that only obvious, logical and safe solutions are selected. The answer is to remain logical, but to avoid throwing the baby out with the bath water by careful questioning and not hurrying to decisions.

Post-it® Note tools can help with convergence; trees and maps are useful for organizing and understanding. The Bottom-up Tree is particularly good for convergence from a large list. The Swap Sort is good for selecting from a shorter list of items.

Who make good convergent thinkers?

- Judges, who weigh up the pros and cons of an argument.
- Researchers, who patiently sift through mounds of data.

You, when you focus on what's important.

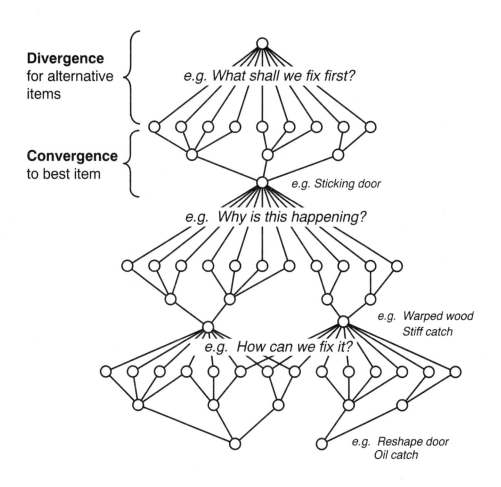

Sequence of divergence and convergence in problem-solving

How chunks fit together

In order to make sense of the many chunks that are created with divergent activities like the Post-up, we begin by looking at how they may be related together. At a basic level, there are three structures we can create: the list, the tree and the map.

Lists

The simplest way to group a number of information chunks is just to list them, one after the other. The Post-up results in a list of chunks, arranged in no particular order. They are related only by the fact that a common set of rules was used to find them all.

The next step beyond the non-ordered list is the ordered list. Take the results of a Post-up or any other tool and ask the question, 'Which is most important?'. Then create a list where the Note at the top is the most important, followed by the next most important and so on down to the least important Note at the bottom. The Swap Sort can be used to produce this prioritized list.

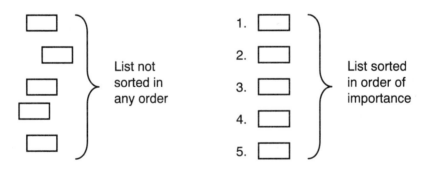

Lists show non-ordered or ordered simple groups

Trees

Chunks are usually made up of other, smaller chunks. Thus a car includes a door, which includes a handle, which includes a lever, and so on.

Chunking works in both directions. Given a piece of information, you can both 'chunk down' by breaking it into its constituent parts, or 'chunk up' by finding what it is a part of. Thus 'casing fractures' may be chunked down to 'stressed in operation' and 'weak joint', or chunked up to 'machine failure'.

Connecting these different levels of chunks together forms a tree-shaped structure, and the two directions of chunking give us the two varieties of tree tool: the Top-down Tree and the Bottom-up Tree.

Trees appear in many situations, because either the situation naturally contains a tree, such as an organizational chart, or this multiple level chunking fits the way our minds work. For example, when writing a book, the main structure may be determined first, followed by chapters, sections and subsections.

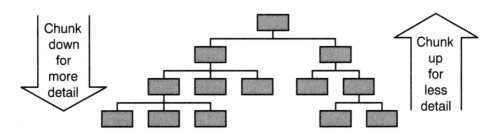

Trees show hierarchical relationships

Maps

In some situations, the information chunks have more complex relationships than can be shown in trees. The human mind is quite good at dealing with this type of situation, fitting random chunks into familiar patterns, often using a known set of rules. For example, when talking with a group of people, we will combine what we know about the topic of conversation with what we know about each person, tempering what we say and how we say it.

Similarly, we can build chunks of information into complex maps to help us understand a situation better. These maps differ from each other, and from hierarchies, in the *type* of relationship between individual chunks. For example, where the chunks are people, the relationship may be one of friendship, of formal reporting line, etc.

A common relationship in maps is between tasks or actions, as shown in the Action Map. The Information Map is used to show any other general relationships, the most common of which is how chunks are caused by other chunks.

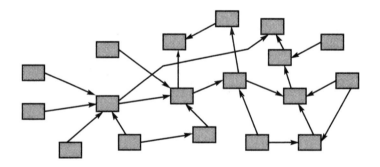

Maps show complex interrelationships

2 Making Decisions

When finding and organizing information chunks, you are continually making decisions. But how do you recognize those decision points? And how do you know if you are making the right decision?

There are two important factors to consider which will help you to make your decisions more effective:

- First, how do you decide what information to collect? How do you know how to put it together? How do you decide which are the important bits? Without some kind of guidance, you can easily make decisions that point you in the wrong direction.
- Second, how true is the information on which you are basing your decisions? If you are using inaccurate information, then your decisions are unlikely to give the right answer. As the saying goes: 'Garbage in, garbage out'.

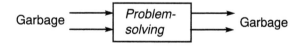

Garbage in = Garbage out

Guiding lights

In order to help you find the right information chunks in a session, to help organize them and to make the right decisions afterwards, you need some kind of direction, some guiding light.

A simple set of guidelines will help you to identify and put together the right information chunks, and then to decide on the right subsequent actions.

Objectives

It has been said that if you aim at nothing, you will probably hit it. You can often see this in problem-solving situations where people are working hard, but do not seem to achieve anything.

The minimum guideline for any activity is that you should write a 'statement of objectives' describing what you are trying to achieve. This provides the main guiding light for all other actions and decisions, and must be clear and concise. It should also be easy to tell when it has been met.

Written objectives are particularly useful when working with other people, as they provide a 'contract of agreement' and ensure that everyone is working in the same direction.

A clear objective:

  Reduce clerical errors on outbound invoices by 50% by the end of May.

An unclear objective:

  Reduce errors.

Criteria

If you ask ten people to select a good piece of music, they will each choose differently because they each judge music by different standards.

You can make better, more acceptable decisions in problem-solving by clarifying your criteria for each decision.

The basic criterion for any decision is that it helps to achieve the objectives. Other criteria form sub-objectives that help the lower-level decisions. For example, if the objective is to 'select a plant to put in the garden', criteria may include 'stays green all year' and 'resistant to greenfly'.

Questions

One of the best ways of directing activities in problem-solving is to ask pertinent questions which give strong direction or act as simple prompts to stimulate further thinking.

Questioning can form the basis of a complete approach to problem-solving (see Chapter 10).

Other guidelines

Other guidelines that can help your decision-making include *non-objectives* that clarify the boundaries of the basic objectives and *constraints* that further limit what you can do.

When writing objectives, criteria and other guidelines, always aim to keep a balance between brevity and detail. The bottom line is that they should *help*, not hinder your decision-making.

The FOG factor

A simple and effective way of identifying the quality of information chunks is to classify them into Facts, Opinions or Guesses. If you take the first letter of each of these words, they spell 'FOG', which provides a useful way of remembering them. (If it is not clear how true a chunk is, your confidence in its use is likely to be pretty foggy.)

Facts

Facts are incontrovertible, and are capable of being proved in a court of law. They are the best form of information, but are surprisingly rare.

The usual way of finding facts is by measuring, which may range from qualitative questioning to quantitative physical measurement. What you measure will depend on the question you want to answer.

Facts are seldom free. To prove that customers like a new product feature, for example, you have to go out and ask them.

Facts are not always expensive. Sometimes a simple check will tell you exactly what you want to know. For example, if you think that a growing medium might be acidic, then you can easily prove it by measuring the pH with a piece of litmus paper.

The key to using facts is to balance the potential benefit of knowing with the cost of finding out. It is easy to fall too far in either direction, either by wasting time on those last few percentage points or by claiming that it is 'just not worth the effort'.

When problem-solving it is important to identify opinions and guesses that, if proven to be facts, are valuable enough to warrant further action.

Opinions

Opinions are the most common form of information. They are the considered thoughts of people, and may well be facts–they just cannot be proved.

Opinions have the widest range of possible truth, as they can range from considerations based on long and practical experience through uncertain hearsay to outright prejudice.

One problem with opinions is that people who have them tend to think of them as facts, even when they are not. If their opinions are respected, then other people may also treat them as facts. Opinions should be recognized as such, and treated with due caution.

An important part of problem-solving lies not only in differentiating between facts and opinions, but also in exploring opinions and finding out how people have come to their conclusions.

Guesses

Guesses, on the other hand, are acknowledged as uncertain ideas. They are given in divergent activities, aimed at expanding the potential area of interest.

They often appear in Post-up sessions where you are deliberately looking for creative new concepts.

Most guesses turn out to be untrue and of little value, so why use them? Because those few that are of value tend to provide a significant breakthrough. Guesses can be the most useless and the most useful part of solving problems.

Using the FOG factor

In problem-solving, consider any chunk by asking, 'What is the FOG Factor?' and then mark it accordingly. With Post-it® Note problem-solving, you can either use different shades of Note (blue = Fact, yellow = Opinion, red = Guess) or write the letters F, O or G in one corner of the Note.

Subsequent activities may then be undertaken to research and perform experiments in order to promote guesses and opinions into facts. For example, a guess that customers might like bright green shoes may be followed by a survey to elicit their opinion and a market pilot to determine the facts about the saleability of such clothes.

Note that not all problem situations require the application of the FOG factor. Where the information chunks identified are of the same type, there is no need to mark all Notes with the same letter–for example, in a creative Post-up where they are all guesses, or in a Top-down Tree where they are all opinions.

FOG factors

- Facts are proven.
- Opinions are believed to be true by individuals.
- Guesses are recognized as uncertain ideas.

Work to convert Opinions and Guesses into Facts.

Part II

The Post-it® Note Toolbox

The Post-it® Note toolbox consists of three classes of tool, each containing two separate tools, as shown in the tree below. The chapters in this part provide easy steps in how to use each tool. Part III then gives some examples of how the tools may be used together to solve actual problems.

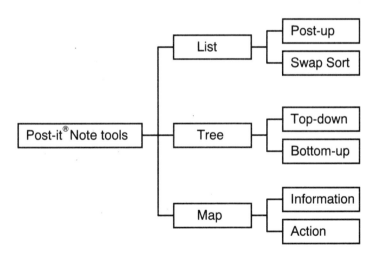

The Post-it® Note Toolbox

Post-it® Note tools

3 Using the Post-it® Note Tools

Whenever you are using Post-it® Note tools to solve problems, there is a common set of actions that may be carried out. Although they are not directly related to any one tool, each step will contribute to the successful use of all tools.

In summary, these steps are:

1. Identify the objective of using the tool.
2. Identify other guidelines to help meet the objective.
3. Determine where the information may be found.
4. Assemble a team to work on the problem.
5. Prepare for the meeting.
6. Use the tool to gather and organize the information.
7. Use the results to achieve the objective.

1. Identify objective

Identify the objective of using the tool by describing, as simply as possible, what you are trying to achieve. For example:

- Find the main causes of customer dissatisfaction.
- Decide what present to give John for his birthday.
- Reduce invoicing costs by 10 per cent.
- Allocate tasks for rebuilding furnaces.

Identifying your objective will help you to decide on other actions whilst using the tool. It also helps you to know when to stop, as no more work is needed when the objective has been met.

2. Identify constraints, etc.

Identify any additional information that may help you keep on the right track. This may include:

- *Constraints*, which limit what you can do. They typically involve cost, time or resource.
- *Non-objectives*–what you are *not* trying to achieve. They might be mistaken for objectives.
- *Questions* to ask yourself when creating and moving Notes. You only get the right answer if you ask the right question.

Examples:
Constraint–Task must be done by end of January and be within current budget.
Non-objective–Reducing space usage (when no extra space is needed).
Question–What is a direct cause of this?

3. Find where the information is held

Determine where the information may be found that will be needed to meet the objective. If it is in reports, minutes, books etc., then take a pad of Post-it® Notes and do some research.

If the information required is not written down or easily available, identify a team of people who can work together on the problem.

4. Select the team

When identifying team members, be sure they can all contribute in some way, and between them have (or have access to) all necessary information.

Try to choose those who will work together well and whose knowledge and thinking style match the problem. Some problems require more creative thinking, whilst others benefit from a more logical approach.

A smaller team is usually more effective than a larger team. Three to four people is good, although up to around ten can work satisfactorily.

Make sure the people are comfortable using the Post-it® Note tools. Separate training may be given or a short presentation in the meeting, followed by close assistance during use may suffice.

Use a facilitator or have at least one person in the group who is reasonably expert in using the tools and is able to show the others what to do. If everyone is new to the tools, be prepared to go more slowly and not to achieve perfect results first time.

5. Set up the working area

In the meeting, set up three vertically mounted areas, as shown in the diagram, that everyone can see and access.

The Help page is typically a flipchart, placed to one side. This contains the objective from Step 1 above, plus any other hints or constraints that will help to focus the team and encourage useful chunks and relationships to be identified.

The Work Area is where the main sticking up of Notes takes place, so it needs to be quite large and central. A whiteboard is good, as it enables lines to be drawn and redrawn between Notes. An alternative, which can be taken away from the meeting room, is several sheets of flipchart paper, taped together.

The Store is simply an area to the side of the Work Area for putting Notes that are not a part of the current diagram. It may contain Notes from an initial Post-up or ones that have been temporarily removed from the Work Area.

When the Work Area starts overflowing, the Store also provides a useful 'secondary' work area in which to continue the diagram. Use letter codes (such as a capital 'A' in a circle) to show the link point in the Work Area and the continuation point in the Store.

As most sessions are highly active, you will need to have sufficient space in front of these areas for everyone to move about freely. There should be pads of Post-it® Notes and marker pens on tables nearby. Arrange chairs in a semicircle further back.

Help

*Objectives,
constraints and
other prompts
to help achieve
an effective
session.*

Store

*Temporary storage of Notes
and a secondary work area.*

Work Area

*The main working area where the Notes
are organized in the session.*

Setting up for Post-it® Note session

6. Use the tool to organize information

Use the tool, as described in the following chapters, to create or organize your information.

7. Use results to meet the objective

After using the tool, spend some time ensuring you have acquired the right information, then use it to achieve your objective.

In creative activities, if you have the time, leave the Notes in place for several days to let ideas 'incubate'. In this period, go back from time to time just to look, adding or changing Notes as desired.

For more logical activities or where you have made assumptions, verify these assumptions by performing various experiments, asking people, taking measurements, etc.

When you are comfortable with the final diagram, put it onto paper and give everyone a copy. It will serve as a concise documentation of the decision-making process you have used, which may be checked when you later succeed (or otherwise) in meeting your objective.

4 The Post-up

What is it for?

To collect pieces of information about a situation.

When do I use it?

To gather discrete chunks of information about a problem situation, particularly when that information is not written down neatly in one place (this happens in most problems!).

It is commonly used where the information is held in people's heads, i.e. where a set of individuals each knows something about a part of the problem, but not all of it.

The Post-up can also be used to collect various written information from reports, documents, journals, etc.

Use it, rather than conventional brainstorming, for easier and quicker generation of creative new ideas.

By itself, the Post-up does nothing with the information that it creates, so use it with other Post-it® Note tools to help make useful decisions, either as an integral part, building a problem structure as you go, or as two separate sessions, first doing a Post-up then using a second tool to organize the results.

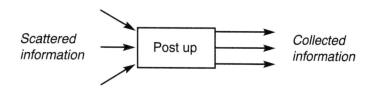

How does it work?

Information about a problem is often scattered and unclear. It may be in various places, such as old reports and meeting minutes, or it may never have been written down and can only be found by asking the right questions of a number of people.

Collecting this information together in one place allows it to be reviewed and understood as a whole, especially if each piece is a uniform and discrete chunk. Once collected, these chunks may then be organized relative to one another to reveal further useful information.

The Post-up involves writing down each piece of information on a Note, then sticking it up with others. The result is a large sheet of paper, a whiteboard or wall which is covered in Notes.

The real value of the Post-up comes when it is used with a team of people, as it actively involves everyone in writing and posting. Compared with traditional brainstorming meetings, where one person stands at the front writing down thoughts as they are called out, the Post-up has several beneficial effects:

- *Efficient use of time*–no one has to wait for their turn before giving suggestions.
- *Effective data collection*–everyone is involved, all of the time. No one can sit back and let the others do the work.
- *Fair play*–no one person dominates. Independent action means everyone is equal.
- *Relative anonymity*–focus on individuals is reduced; focus on the problem is increased.

Minimizing talk during the Post-up session contributes to all of the above, allowing each person to concentrate on the task in hand. It also helps in creative sessions, where it encourages the use of the non-verbal, creative parts of the brain.

The Post-up also recognizes that you may not collect all the information you need in one session, and thus allows for an 'incubation' period during which new Post-it® Notes may be added.

The Post-up

How do I do it?

1. Identify objective

Identify your objective, and set up the meeting as described in Chapter 3. Here are some typical Post-up objectives:

- How can the cassette case be made 10 per cent thinner?
- What is the factual (not circumstantial) evidence in the case of burglary Ref. RQ142?
- What boys' names do we like?
- What do we know about the Corvan release plans?

In a creative session, the following considerations may help:

- Hold it somewhere informal, outside the normal working environment.
- Don't invite people who will inhibit the others (e.g. the boss).
- Stimulate the creative juices beforehand with a game.
- Add 'thought trigger' questions to the Help area to prompt creative thinking. They can be single words or longer sentences or phrases, for example:
  - Replace?
  - Extend?
  - Rearrange?
  - Reduce or simplify?
  - Combine items?
  - Change the sequence?

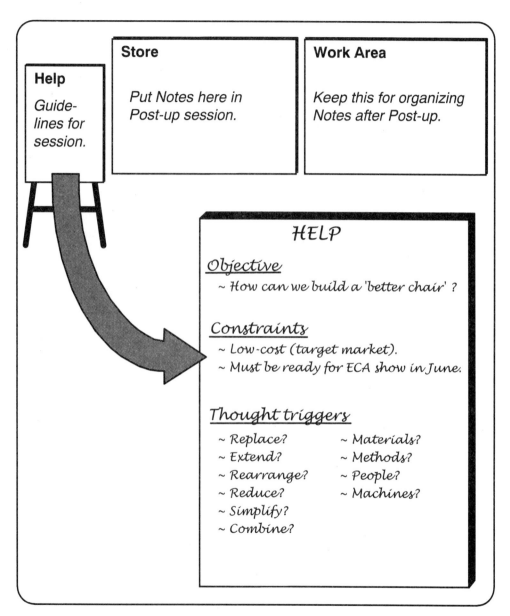

Setting up for the Post-up session

2. All stick Post-it® Notes in the Store

Give each person a Post-it® Note pad and a marker pen, then proceed with the Post-up, as follows:

- Each participant writes statements or phrases that help to answer the question from step 1, putting one statement on one note. They then stick it up on the Store. (The Work Area is kept clear for organizing the notes afterwards, using another tool.)
- If the Notes contain a mixture of facts, opinions and guesses, then these differences should be indicated, either by using different shades of Note (blue = Fact, yellow = Opinion, red = Guess) or by writing the letter F, O or G in the top righthand corner of each Note. A fact can be proved, an opinion is believed to be true, a guess is simply an idea.
- No talking is allowed during the Post-up. The only exception may be an occasional question to clarify the meaning of something written on a Note.
- Keep stimulating yourselves for new things to post:
  - Look at other Notes.
  - Look at the objectives and questions on the Help area.
  - Take a break then come back afresh.

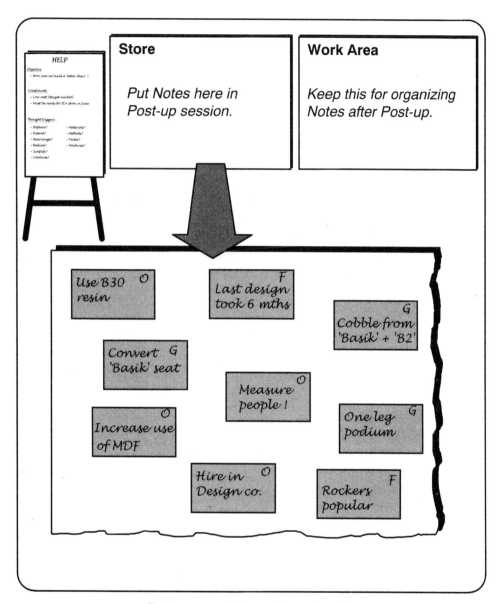

Posting up information chunks

3. Use the results as planned

When everyone has run out of ideas to post up, either close the session or move on to using the Post-up Notes with another tool.

If you have the time, it is often a good idea to leave the Post-up in place for a few days. Return to it over the next week or so, adding new Notes as more information is found or ideas appear. If appropriate, you can even leave it in a public place, encouraging visitors to add their own thoughts.

This 'incubation period' also allows the validity of thoughts and ideas to sink in before making further judgments on them.

Post-up Keys

- Guiding objectives and questions clearly shown nearby.
- One phrase or statement per Note. Make it easy for everyone to understand.
- Discriminate between facts, opinions and guesses.
- Everyone works together. Write a Note and stick it up.
- Once a Note is posted, leave it. They can be moved or removed later.
- Silence. Talking removes focus from the Post-up.
- Look at other Notes and think. Key off other people's thoughts.
- When everyone is done, leave it up. Keep coming back to add more.

5 The Swap Sort

What is it for?

To prioritize a list of items.

When do I use it?

When you have a disorganized list of items that you want to sort into an order of importance, for example where you have a list of possible actions and you want to select only one or two to carry forward.

A short list of items (around ten or less) is best as it can be time-consuming when used to sort a long list. Long lists can be used, provided they are reduced as described.

The Swap Sort is very useful when a group of people cannot agree on which items are most important. It forces them to tackle the problem in a more organized manner.

It is typically used after other Post-it® Note tools, either directly after a Post-up or when a shorter list has been selected from a Tree or Map.

Collected information → Swap Sort → Prioritized and selected information

How does it work?

A common situation when working on a problem is where you have a number of information chunks which you want either to put into some order of importance or to select one or two to carry forward for future action. For example, you may first find many ideas on how to reduce insect infestation, but how do you then choose the best one to use?

This problem is addressed with the Swap Sort, which puts a disorganized list of items into order of importance.

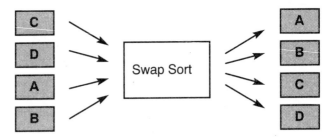

Before starting to find this priority order, you must ask, 'What makes one item more important than another?' Different people may use different criteria and will consequently disagree about the importance of each item. To avoid this, you must agree on a list of selection criteria as a consistent way of judging each item.

The Swap Sort works simply by repeatedly comparing pairs of Notes in a list, then swapping them if they are in the wrong positions. Comparing in pairs against a defined criteria makes the decision of 'which is more important' much easier and more likely to give good results than simply plucking the Notes out of a large group.

If the list is almost in order, few swaps will be needed. Conversely, a list in reverse order can require rather more swaps before it is sorted out. The maximum number of swaps increases sharply with the number of items in the list, as shown in the table below, which effectively limits the size of the list. It is thus quicker to shorten a long list before starting to swap.

Number of items in list	Maximum number of swaps
2	1
3	3
5	10
10	45
20	190

Swap Sort

How do I do it?

1. Identify objective

Identify your objective, and set up the meeting as described in Chapter 3. Some typical objectives include:

- Select probable causes of engine failure to investigate.
- Decide which articles to write, and in which order.
- Find the winner of the violin competition.
- Identify features to include in the new product.

2. Create prioritization criteria

Use the objective from Step 1 to create the prioritization criteria which will be used when comparing the Notes to judge which are more important. Typical criteria are:

- Costs little to implement.
- Easy to do (we have the skills).
- Follows the defined standards or rules.
- Quick to do.
- No need to involve other people (do it ourselves).
- Easy to persuade other people.

Phrase the criteria to make agreeing with them desirable–'quick to implement' rather than 'speed of implementation'.

There should be very few criteria. One is ideal, three are acceptable, more will make later decisions increasingly difficult.

Where the criteria and *their* order of importance are not clear, you can use a mini Post up and Swap Sort to find and sort them into order (using the objective to compare them).

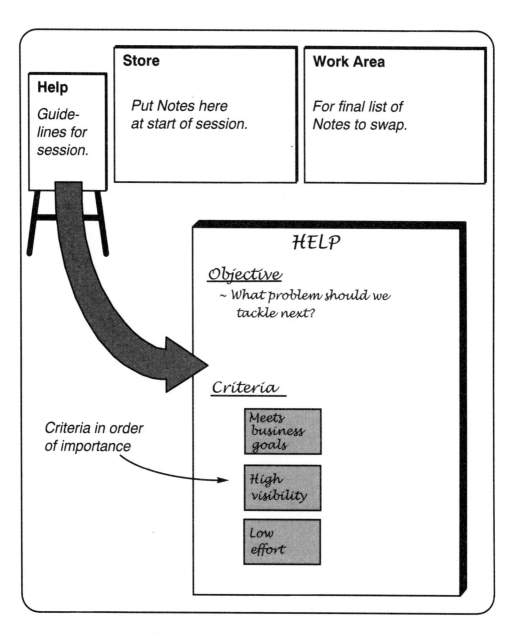

Setting up criteria for Swap Sort

3. Gather Notes

Gather the items you want to sort, each written on one Note, and put them in the Store area. They may come from a Post-up or a selection of key items from a Tree or Map.

4. Reduce size of long lists

If there are more than about ten Notes to sort, reduce them as follows:

- Compare each Note against the objective and criteria. Decide whether it is worth keeping, or may be rejected now as a low priority item. If it is worth keeping, transfer it to the Work Area.
- Look for pairs of Notes which are effectively duplicates or may be combined. Either put one Note to one side or stick both Notes together.

Another way of quickly reducing even a very large list is to ask everyone to select a fixed number of Notes (e.g. five) to carry forward into a new, smaller list. If necessary, repeat several times to shorten the list further.

5. Arrange in a vertical list

Arrange Notes in the Work Area into a vertical list. (They will be sorted into order of importance in the next step, so don't try to sort them now!)

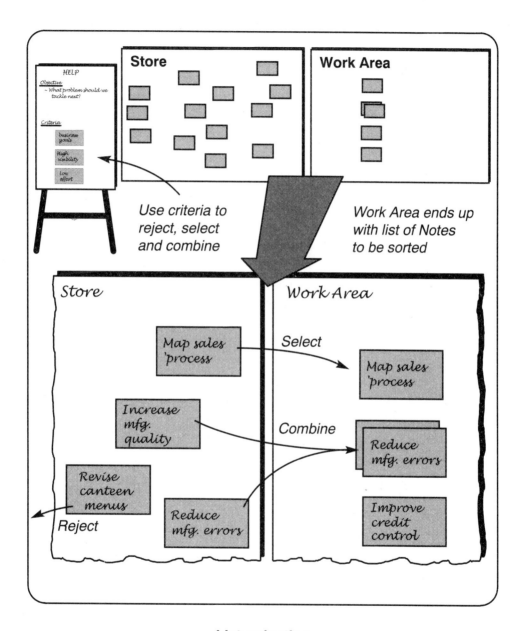

List reduction

6. Swap pairs of Notes

Compare and swap pairs of Notes using the following process:

- Compare the first two Notes at the top of the list, using the criteria from Step 2. If the lower one is more important than the higher one, then swap their positions in the list.
- Compare the next two Notes in the list (including the second in the list, which you just compared, plus the next Note down, number three in the list). As in the previous comparison, if they are in the wrong order, swap them.
- Repeat this comparing and swapping of Notes until you reach the bottom of the list. If there are five Notes in the list, you will compare one and two, then two and three, then three and four, then four and five.
- If any pair of Notes was swapped in this pass through the list, repeat the process and keep repeating it until you can go through the complete list without swapping any pairs.

Thus, the sequence for sorting a list of letters could look like this:

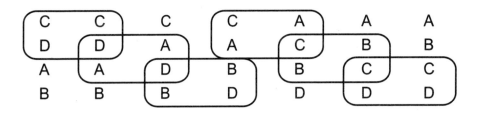

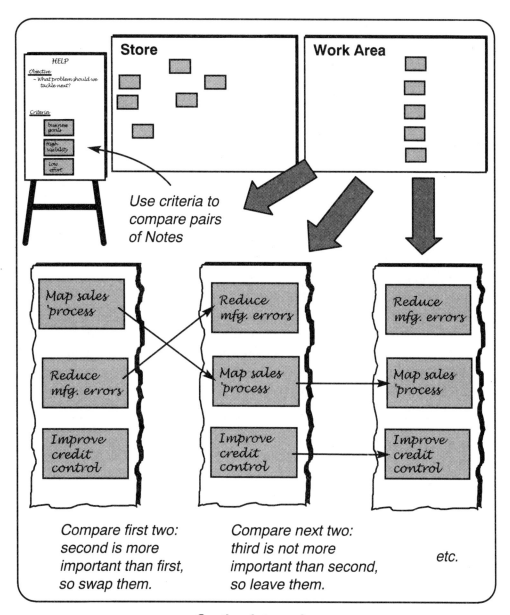

Use criteria to compare pairs of Notes

Compare first two: second is more important than first, so swap them.

Compare next two: third is not more important than second, so leave them.

etc.

Sorting into order

7. Use list as planned

The Notes are now in order of importance, according to your criteria. Use the list as identified in your original objective.

Swap Sort Keys

- Agree on what 'important' means.
- Reduce the list to ten Notes or less.
- Put the Notes vertically above one another.
- Compare pairs of Notes (starting from the top and working down).
- If the lower Note of a pair is more important than the higher one, then swap their positions in the list.
- Repeat the process until you can't find any more pairs to swap.

---

6 The Top-down Tree

What is it for?

To break down a problem into a useful set of parts.

When do I use it?

When investigating a problem, or an interesting part of it, where you can describe the problem with a simple statement.

When designing something, from a house to an essay, it is useful to identify the individual components. Similarly, with an existing item such as a competitor's product, you can discover how it is made.

Another common use is trying to find out why something is happening. In this case use the tree to identify possible causes of a known effect. You can also reverse this process when looking for possible solutions to a problem, finding out how a desired effect may be caused.

Yet another application is when planning a project, breaking down large tasks into units that can easily be allocated and managed.

Use it instead of a Bottom-up Tree when the general problem is known and you want to find more detail, rather than the other way around.

Use it, instead of an Information Map, to do a logical breakdown of the problem, rather than a more creative investigation of relationships.

How does it work?

There are many situations where you have a small amount of information, possibly only a simple description of the problem. You then need to find out more detail about the problem, to expand upon it or to dig down until useful information underneath is found.

The Top-down Tree breaks down a single problem chunk into layers of more detailed chunks by repeatedly asking a simple defined question. It enables you to build up a consistent and complete picture of the problem. Also, as only one chunk is dealt with at one time, it can make a complex problem much easier to handle.

When you are working on a problem with clear boundaries, using a structured set of questions to break down the tree helps to ensure that the complete problem, no more and no less, is mapped.

The Top-down Tree can help improve your appreciation of a problem. As you are breaking down the tree, the effect of 'unfolding' the problem one level at a time allows you to explore and understand it better than if you had gone straight into the detail. Like peeling an onion, each layer can be carefully examined, one at a time, before going down to the next.

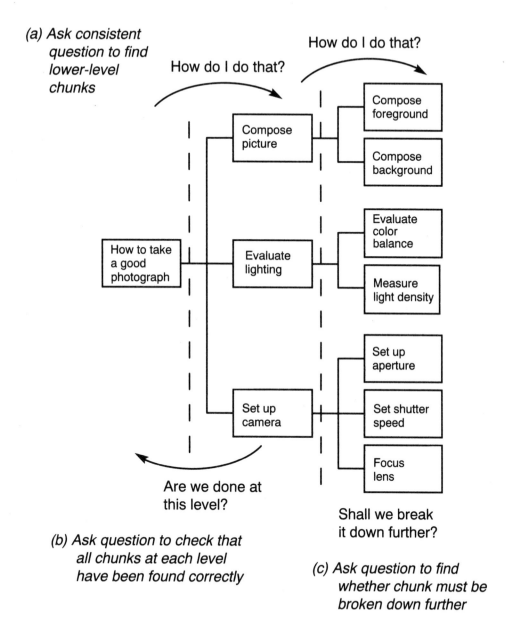

Top-down Tree

There are a number of words commonly used to describe different parts of a tree, most of them derived either from parts of a family tree or from parts of the more familiar, wooden variety.

- A single item is sometimes called a *node* (the lumpy bit on a plant or tree where the leaf joins the main stem).
- The one top-level node is called the *root*, as all other items stem from this.
- A *parent* has one or more *children* items beneath it.
- A *child* has one parent only. All nodes except the root are children. This parent–child structure is known as a *hierarchy*, and distinguishes trees from maps.
- A *leaf* is a bottom-level node that has no children of its own.
- All children of one parent are often (but not always) considered together as a *family*, as in combination they are equivalent to the parent. In such cases, all leaves together represent the root.

  For example, if the tree is used to break down a vehicle into its sub-assemblies and parts, the leaves will contain all the individual components that are required to build the original vehicle.

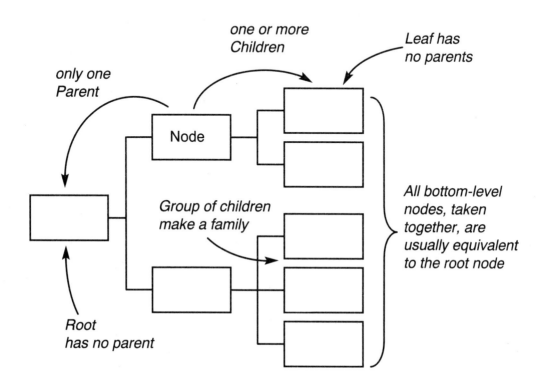

Parts of a Tree

Whichever way the tree is built, the result is always a hierarchy, although there are a number of different ways that this can be laid out. The approach you take can depend on the type of problem you are solving, the space available for sticking up Notes, or may be a case of individual preference.

This book consistently uses a left-to-right layout, but there is no reason why you should not use any of the other possible approaches. Do your own experiments, using the table below to help decide which methods best suit your problem-solving situations.

Tree shape	When tree may be useful
Left-to-right	Easy to distinguish levels, but may run out of vertical space when there are many children in families.
Top-down	Sufficient for simple trees, but may run out of horizontal space, especially in a narrow work area. Combine with a comb when there are many leaves.
Comb	Useful with a long narrow work area (such as several separate flipchart sheets).
Inside-out	Useful layout for the Bottom-up Tree. Not recommended for Top-down Tree.
Fishbone	A flexible variant of left-to-right, but families in middle of diagram may run out of space.
Star	Useful when there are many children at each level, but can become messy when families start to merge.

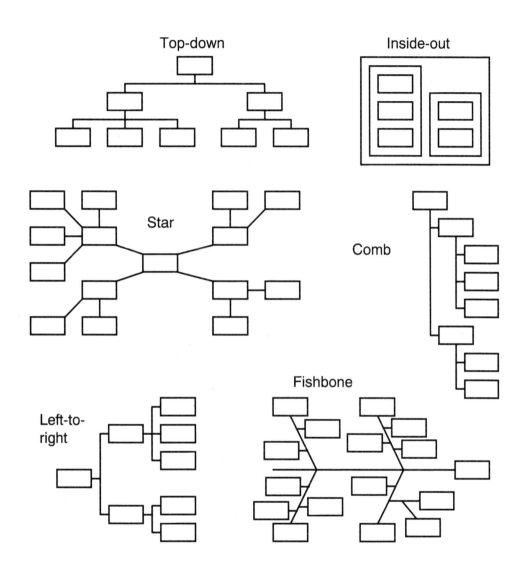

Tree Layouts

How do I do it?

1. Identify objectives

Identify objectives and people, and set up the meeting as described in Chapter 3. Some typical objectives are:

- Find key reasons why wood in storage shed B is warping.
- Define the roles needed in the new organization.
- Identify tasks for assembly of Maximan radio.

2. Identify 'Help' questions

Use the objective to identify questions to ask while building the tree, then write these in the Help Area. There are three questions you can use:

(a) To ask of a parent that will help you identify its children. For example, 'What would directly cause this?'

(b) To ask of children to check they have all been correctly identified. For example, 'Do all children, taken together, completely represent the parent?'

(c) To ask of a Note, to determine whether you need to find its children. When the answer is 'no' for all childless Notes, you have completed the tree. For example, 'Can this task be completed within one week?' or 'Do I need to know more detail?'

It can sometimes be useful to change question (a) at a defined point in the tree. For example, 'What causes this?' until no more causes can be found, then changing to 'How can it be fixed?'

Help
Guide-
lines for
session.

Store

Put spare Notes
here during session.

Work Area

Build tree here
during session.

HELP

Objective
~ What is causing marks on
   copier printed sheets?

Questions
First layer:
   Identify : What parts could cause
              marking?
   Check : Are all parts identified?

Subsequent layers:
   Identify : How could marking
              happen?
   Check : Are all alternatives
           identified?

*Finished when no more causes found,
plus 1 week's incubation period.*

Objectives and questions

3. Write root problem statement

Use the objective from Step 1 to write a clear and unambiguous problem statement or question on a Note. This forms the root Note of the tree. For example, an objective of, 'Identify causes of workroom overheating' may result in a root problem of 'workroom is overheating'.

Stick this up in the Work Area in a position where the rest of the tree can flow from away from it. Where you put it will depend how you intend to shape the tree (see page 51).

4. Identify children

Identify the children of the root Note by asking question (a) from Step 2. Write each child item on one Note and stick it up in the Work Area, near the root problem, but spaced widely enough for subsequent children to be positioned.

Ask question (b) from step 2 to find out whether you have completed the family. If not, then keep asking questions.

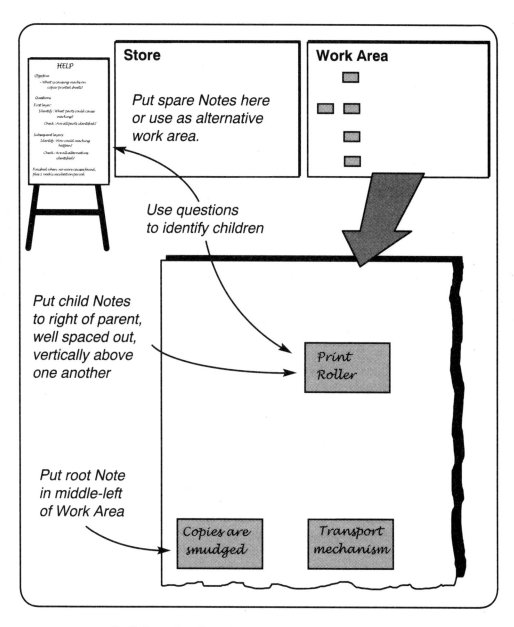

Building the first level of the Top-down Tree

5. Check for completion

For each child identified in Step 4, ask question (c) from Step 2 in order to decide whether more children need to be found. If they do, identify and position them in the Work Area as in Step 4.

Repeat this process identifying one complete family at a time until there are no more children to find.

When breaking down a tree, aim for small families as they are easier to arrange and to understand. Large families at any one level can be caused by multiple levels being squashed together. Ask of each Note, 'Should this be at a lower level? Is it directly related to the parent?'

When sticking up Notes, make sure that they are positioned such that individual families can be clearly identified with sufficient space around each Note for *its* children to be positioned.

If families collide or you run out of space to position Notes, then rearrange the tree, either by shuffling Notes, moving out entire sub-trees or by rebuilding the sub-tree in the Store area.

Sometimes, rearranging Notes becomes rather awkward, either because you are running out of space in which to reorganize or because there are a large number of Notes to move. In this case, use a marker pen to clarify relationships. You can include solid lines between related Notes, reference links to remote sub-trees and dashed lines to separate different families.

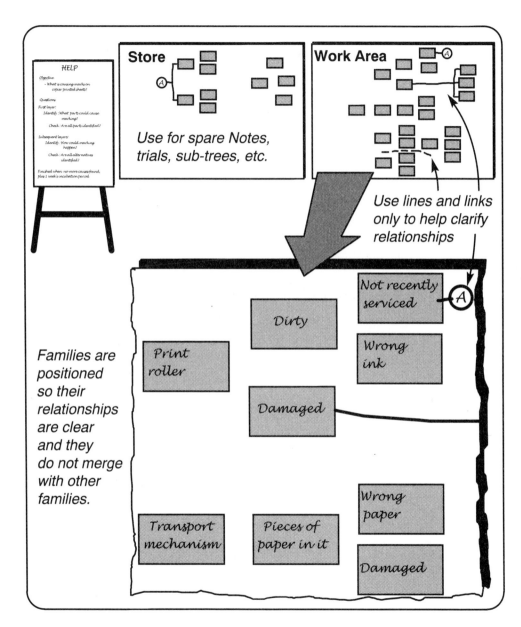

Building up the Tree

6. Add lines

Whilst the structure of the tree is still uncertain, avoid adding lines if you can. However, when you are confident that the tree is correct, then add lines to highlight the family groups.

In case you do have to move Notes, use a whiteboard for the Work Area to make it easier to erase old lines.

Adding lines gives the tree a greater sense of completeness, as the structure can now be clearly seen. It also can make you feel less ready to change the tree, which is another reason for leaving this step until the end.

Where sub-trees have been continued elsewhere, such as in the Store area, show the link to them with a circle at both the 'jump out' and 'arrive in' points, with each circle containing the same unique letter.

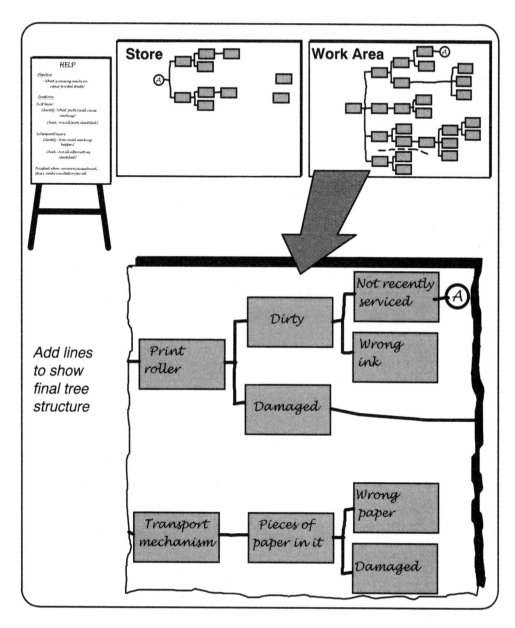

Adding links to Top-down Tree

7. Check completed tree

When the tree is finished, review it for completeness, clarity and usefulness as follows:

Completeness	Check that questions from Step 2 are fully and correctly answered at each layer.
Clarity	Ensure that both individual Notes and relationships between parents and children are easily understood.
Usefulness	Ask whether the completed tree can be used to meet the objective from Step 1.

Put an appropriate amount of effort into this step, depending on the importance of the final results. For example, use extra effort in reviewing a breakdown of tasks in a mission-critical project.

Top-down Tree Keys

- Define questions to help you identify children, check families and decide when the tree is complete.
- Choose a tree shape. If unsure, use Left-to-right.
- Write one item per Note, starting with the root problem.
- Identify children by consistently ask a defined question.
- Position Note families so relationships are clear.
- Move Notes or use a marker pen if relationships become unclear.
- Add lines at end to show families.

7 The Bottom-up Tree

What is it for?

To organize many diverse chunks of information into a clear and coherent whole.

When do I use it?

When there are many individual pieces of information about a problem and it is not clear how they are related. The information chunks need not all be clear and written down; they can be vague and half-thought-out. It is the job of the Bottom-up Tree to help make sense of this confusion.

This often happens when you are just starting to find out about a problem and are trying to piece together the bits of the jigsaw from the assorted scraps of knowledge that various people have.

The Bottom-up Tree is useful in formal planning and investigation activities which often start with vague thoughts and ideas as well as in general problem-solving.

Another use is when you have been working on a problem for a while and the tree or map that you are using does not seem to help or reflect the true situation. In this case, the Bottom-up Tree can be used to restructure the information to give a fresh picture of the problem.

It is also useful in a group of people whose individuals cannot agree what the real problem is, as they work on shared data and reach joint conclusions about the problem.

How does it work?

It is very common in problem-solving to have plenty of information, yet still not be any closer to the solution. You cannot see the wood for the trees, as the quantity or diversity of your pieces of information seem more like a confusing labyrinth than a clear path to a solution.

The Bottom-up Tree organizes this mess by grouping these leaves into families, then grouping those families into larger families, and so on until all of the original pieces of information are related together in a tree.

As with the Post-up, when working in a group of people, the tree is usually built in silence. This prevents diversions, such as arguments about where individual Notes should be placed, and other side discussions which are not focused on the problem in hand. It can also help when trying to look afresh at a stuck problem, as it encourages the creative right brain to come to the fore and find hidden, non-obvious ways of grouping Notes.

A Bottom-up Tree will often be fairly shallow, with a few, large families, and only two or three levels. Despite this, there are no rules that say it should not be broken down into more levels with smaller families.

A good Bottom-up Tree will typically take between 25 and 100 seemingly unrelated Notes and find common threads that can be used to weave together a new structure and throw light on a hitherto poorly understood problem.

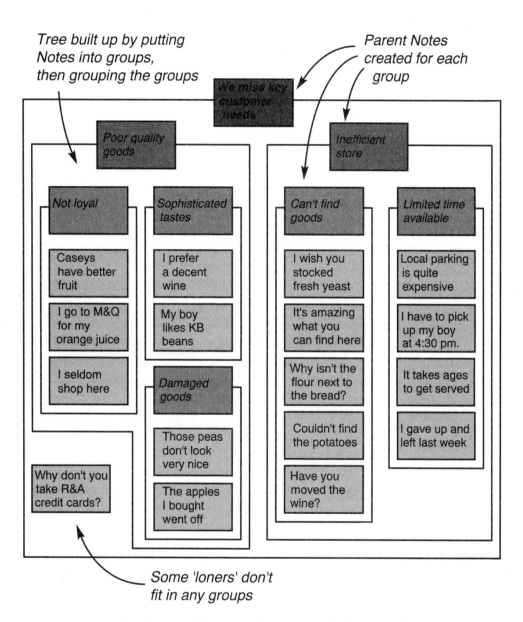

Bottom-up Tree for 'Customer Comments'

How do I do it?

1. Identify objective

Identify your objective and set up the meeting as described in Chapter 3. Some typical objectives are:

- Discover the real problem behind all the complaints we are receiving from the sales force.
- Find out how I perceive the world by grouping a large set of possible needs and wants.
- The whole team is to work together on an action plan for the new product development. The plan is to include all known commitments.

Where the main problem is vague, word the objective in similarly general terms, to 'widen the net' and encourage more creative ideas to be generated. For example:

- Should we replace machines more frequently?
- Making an impact at the exhibition.
- What's bugging the printing division?

The Bottom-up Tree is primarily a method for *discovering* how a set of individual information chunks fit together. It is thus less structured than the Top-down Tree and need not have any further questions in the Help Area. Constraints or triggers can, of course, be added if this will help to achieve your objective.

Help

*Guide-
lines for
session.*

Store

*Start with Notes
here (possibly from
Post-up during session).*

Work Area

*Move Notes here
during session to build
Bottom-up Tree.*

*Only the objective is
given as a guideline
when you want to
be more open to
new thought*

HELP

Objective
~ *What are the issues around
installing a new computer?*

Triggers
~ *What Notes feel like they fit
together? (not just logical
connections).*

Objectives and questions

2. Collect information chunks

Use the objective from Step 1 to guide a Post-up session, collecting individual chunks of information about the problem and sticking these up anywhere in the Store area.

Each Note should be worded so that it can be read and understood by itself, with only the objective to give it context. The Note may contain few words, but often will be a more complete phrase or sentence. If the information is only a half-thought or vague concept, it may still be worth including, particularly if you are investigating an uncertain or creative situation.

Depending on the type of information that you are collecting, the Post-up may be a fairly fast session, completed in a single meeting, or may be a longer process, lasting days or even weeks.

3. Shuffle the Notes

When the Post-up from Step 2 is completed, shuffle the Notes in the Store area by swapping random pairs. This is to break up patterns where a person has followed an existing train of thought and put several logically related Notes close together. It is easier to see new patterns in a random layout than in one where strong patterns already exist.

4. Put columns in Work Area

Use a marker pen to divide the Work Area into columns that are a bit wider than the Notes. If you are using standard flipchart paper, then each sheet divides conveniently into four columns.

Typically, you will need around six to ten columns. If in doubt, start with a lower number and add more as necessary.

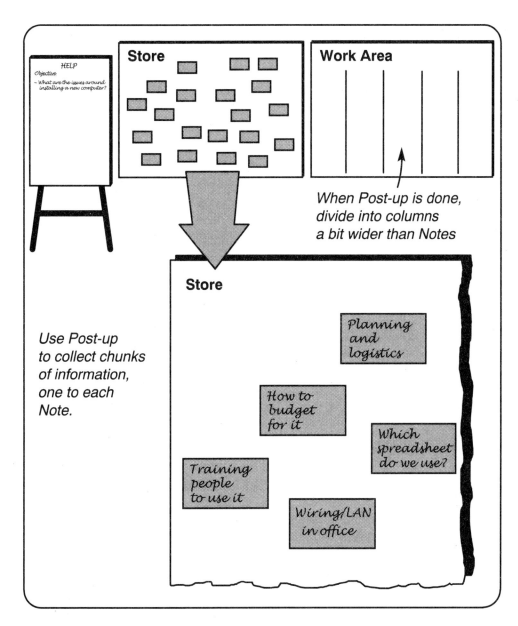

Store

Work Area

HELP
Objective
~ What are the issues around installing a new computer?

When Post-up is done, divide into columns a bit wider than Notes

Store

Use Post-up to collect chunks of information, one to each Note.

Planning and logistics

How to budget for it

Which spreadsheet do we use?

Training people to use it

Wiring/LAN in office

Use a Post-up to collect information

5. Move Notes into columns

Carefully read the Notes in the Store, initially looking for a pair that seem to be related in some way. When two are found, move them both into a single column in the Work Area.

Continue by repeatedly looking in the Store, either for pairs to start new Work Area columns or for single Notes that fit with existing Note groups in the Work Area. Move these across to the appropriate column in the Work Area.

As with the Post-up, everyone does this at the same time, each working independently and silently. It may appear to be a rather chaotic approach, but in practice it works remarkably well.

At first, you will probably be intent upon building your own columns, but as Notes in the Store area begin to run out or there are no obvious Notes to move across, look at the columns that other people have been working on. If you can find Notes to move across to their columns, then do so.

A further step is to 'steal' Notes from other columns. If someone moves a Note away from where you think it should be, look at the column where they moved it to, and ask yourself if that is a better place to put it. If you still think it should be where it was, move it back. This can result in silent 'battle', with Notes being moved back and forth. If it looks like stalemate, write a duplicate, adding 'D' to indicate this.

If a new piece of information occurs to you as you are moving Notes, write it on a new Note and put it either in the Store or in an appropriate column.

Do not have too many Notes in one column. If more than about seven to ten appear together, look for ways of splitting them into two columns.

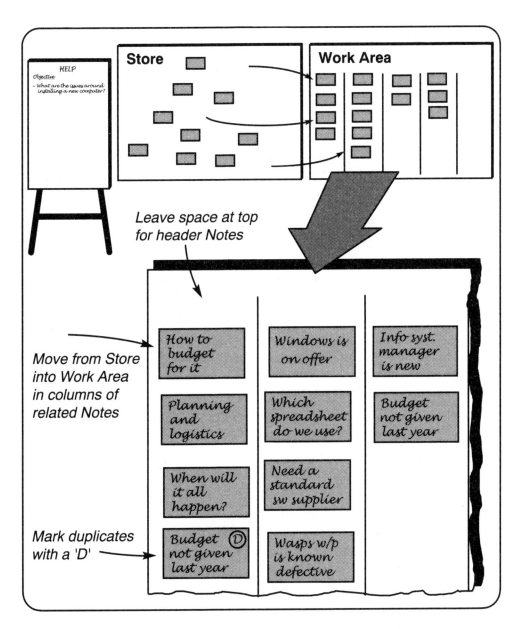

Building up the tree

6. Add header Notes to columns

Eventually the moving of Notes will slow and stop. Don't worry if you still have several Notes in the Store, as this step will find homes for them.

Take each column in turn and discuss the Notes in it, aiming to understand the common factor between them.

When the meaning of the column is agreed, write a header Note for the column, using a different shade of either Note or pen to differentiate it from the other Notes in the column. Stick this at the top of the column.

This discussion is often very illuminating and results in Notes being moved between columns as people realize and agree on the best groupings. You may even want to merge or split columns as the groupings become clearer.

Keep an eye on any Notes left in the Store, looking to move these to columns as headers are written and you improve your understanding of both individual columns and the main problem structure. You should end up with no Notes left in the Store–if necessary, put them in columns containing a single Note.

7. Repeat to organise header Notes

Make a second copy of each header Note, and repeat the above process, putting them into columns and adding header Notes.

Repeat until you have one 'root' header Note which summarizes the whole problem.

As this step is usually quite short, it can be done by discussion, rather than in silence. Depending on the problem, it may also be reasonable for the root header to be directly above the headers from Step 6 (so there is no need to duplicate them).

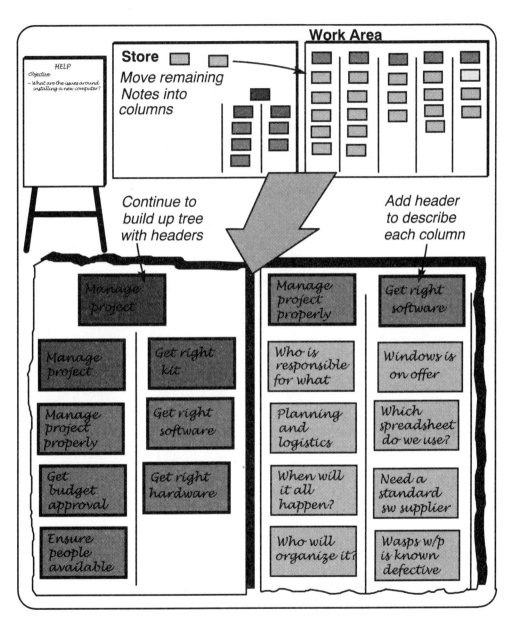

Building up the tree

8. Check completed tree

When the tree is completed, stand back and re-read it. Ask questions to check that it will help achieve the original objective.

If it was done in a 'stuck' project, did you use creative new ways to organize Notes, or old, familiar groupings?

When you are happy with it, you may want to redraw it in a different tree format taken from the illustration on Page 51.

Bottom-up Tree Keys

- Use a Post-up to collect the information chunks.
- Move the Notes into columns of related items.
- Keep moving them between columns until you have finished sorting them.
- Discuss columns and add header Notes to summarize each column.
- Discuss how headers relate and form them into groups, adding a header Note for groups of headers.
- Add a 'root' header Note to summarize top-level headers.

8 The Information Map

What is it for?

To show complex relationships between information chunks.

When do I use it?

When investigating a problem where you know or suspect that the chunks of information are related to one another in a complex, many-to-many manner.

It is particularly useful for non-structured, creative sessions, for example by simply playing with the results of a Post-up and rearranging the Notes to see if any patterns begin to emerge.

Use it when you are investigating interrelated causes in a particularly messy problem.

Information Maps concern *understanding*, and can be used to answer questions like, 'What is the real cause of this problem?'

Use it instead of a tree when the relationship between information chunks is complex, rather than a simple parent-child hierarchy. You may have already tried to use a tree and failed because of the non-hierarchic relationships (one of the benefits of using Notes is that they can simply be rearranged into a Map without rewriting them).

Use it, rather than an Action Map, for more general situations which are not about planning projects or mapping processes.

How does it work?

Many problems have a messy and complex structure, where any individual information chunk may have some relationship to any other chunk. The Information Map is a tool that you can use to discover and demonstrate this picture, by laying out the information chunks and drawing links between them.

The relationship between two information chunks often flows in one direction only. For example, freezing weather may cause ice on the road, but ice does not cause freezing weather. Use arrows to show this directed relationship.

Directed relationship

Arrows may have different meanings in different maps, but in the same map, they usually have only one meaning, such as 'causes', 'belongs to' or 'is near'. Thus all you need to know to start interpreting a map is what the arrow means (which should always be clearly defined).

Information Maps may not show *all* possible relationships, which could result in the key relationships in which you are interested becoming obscured. A consistent approach to identifying relationships, such as asking a standard question, will ensure that only the key arrows that will help you meet your objective of using the map are shown.

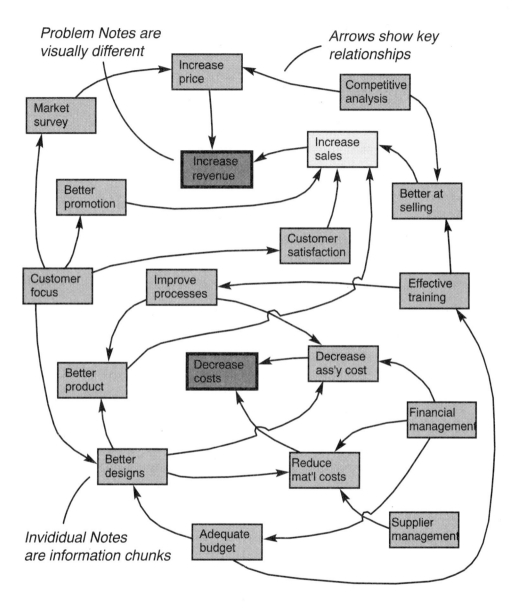

Information Map

The Information Map usually starts with one or more 'problem', or *root* Notes. The Map can also have several points of interest, which may prompt significant decisions to be made, for example:

- *Chains* of Notes, with one arrow between each–e.g. a nail on the road causes a puncture, which causes the vehicle to swerve, which causes an accident. This direct relationship means that removing the nail at the start of chain will also prevent the accident at the end of the chain from happening.
- *Bottlenecks*, where many arrows flow into a single Note, but very few arrows leave it–e.g. several major roads pass through a single town, resulting in traffic chaos and tailbacks.
- *Sources*, where arrows only flow out of a Note–e.g. a government agency provides regular information to various different organizations. In practice, there are few real sources, as even the government agency must get its information from somewhere. In an Information Map, sources typically lie at the edge of the problem, and you are not interested in investigating beyond them.
- *Sinks*, where arrows only flow into a Note–e.g. documents are placed into a central filing system. The root Note may well be a sink.

A 'chain' has several
Notes with one
arrow between each

The Map is started
with one or more
'root' Notes

A 'source' has no
arrows entering it

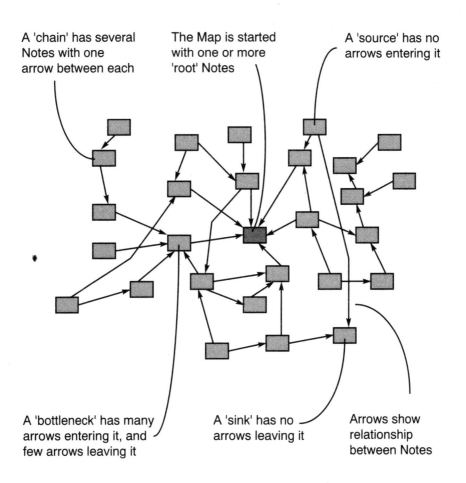

A 'bottleneck' has many
arrows entering it, and
few arrows leaving it

A 'sink' has no
arrows leaving it

Arrows show
relationship
between Notes

Parts of a Map

Notice the difference between the links on a tree and on a map: on a tree, the lines group a whole family together, whilst on a map, one line shows the relationship between only two chunks of information.

The complex relationships between Notes that maps may show also mean that the layout of the map is likely to be less clearly structured than a tree. As a result, maps can be more difficult to interpret, and hence need more care in their construction if they are to be shown to other people.

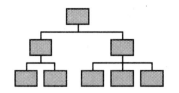

*Relationships between Notes in
a tree are clear from the structure*

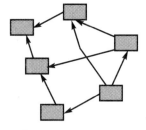

*A map needs arrows to show
the relationship structure*

Tree structure versus Map structure

Building the map

How do I do it?

1. Identify objective

Identify your objective and set up the meeting as described in Chapter 3. Some example objectives are:

- Find the main causes of printer failure.
- Understand how the major roads in the region interconnect.
- Find the informal interpersonal network in the office.

2. Identify mapping guidelines

Use the objective to identify one direct question to ask of each Note that will help find the other Notes that are connected to it. Questions for the above example objectives may be:

- What directly causes this?
- Which roads does this connect to?
- Who knows this person socially?

The question will highlight the verb or verb phrase that describes the arrows between each Note. For example:

- causes
- connects to
- is friends with.

Also identify any constraints that may be used to help select Notes and arrows more precisely, for example:
- LaserJet 4Xi only.
- A-class roads only.
- Full-time employees who work in the finance office and who have social contact with each other.

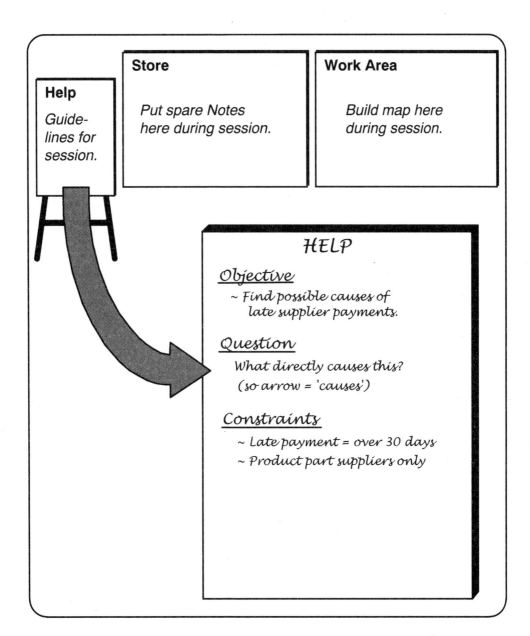

Objectives and questions

3. Identify root Note

Use the information on the Help page to write a clear and unambiguous root Note from which to start the map. This may be a statement describing a problem or any other relevant information. For example, the objective 'Determine factors affecting product cost envelope' may result in a root Note of 'Product cost envelope'.

To make this Note stand out from the others, use a different shade of Note or marker pen.

Stick up the root Note in the middle of the Work Area, in a position where the rest of the map can be built up around it.

There may be more than one root Note. For example when mapping out the supplier chains to a set of company divisions, there would be one Note for each 'root' division, with multiple other Notes, one per supplier.

4. Identify related Notes

Identify the direct relatives of a root Note by asking the question from Step 2. Write each related item on one Note and stick them up in the Work Area, spaced around the root problem Note.

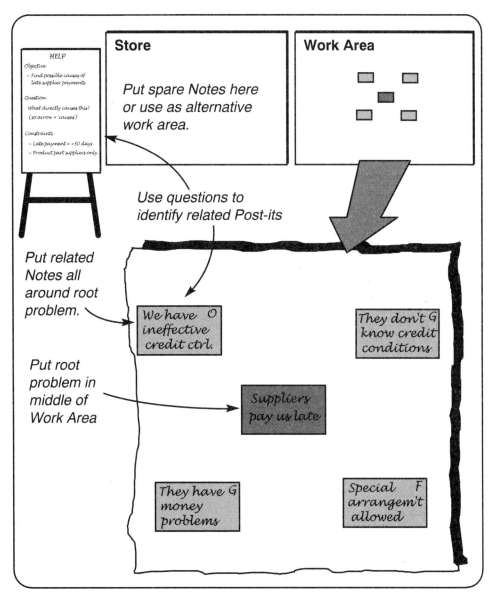

Building the Information Map

5. Repeat to find more Notes

For each Note identified in step 4, find new related information chunks by repeating the process of asking the questions from Step 2.

Position these new Notes around the Note to which they are related. If they appear to be related to other Notes, position them between their relations so it will be easier to add arrows later.

When all related chunks have been added around a Note, add a tick to it. This will help to identify Notes that have not yet been processed, and is especially useful when the diagram becomes more complex.

When sticking up Notes, leave enough space between them to allow arrows to run. When a relationship is found between two distant Notes, the connecting arrow must run around all Notes between them.

If Notes become too bunched up, so that it is difficult to add new ones, rearrange them to give more space. You can also rearrange Notes as new relationships between individual and groups are discovered.

An alternative or supplement to identifying new Notes as you are building the map is to do a Post-up beforehand. The Notes may also come from a 'failed' Top-down Tree, where it is realized that an Information Map is a more appropriate tool. In either case, put the Notes in the Store and select them as required.

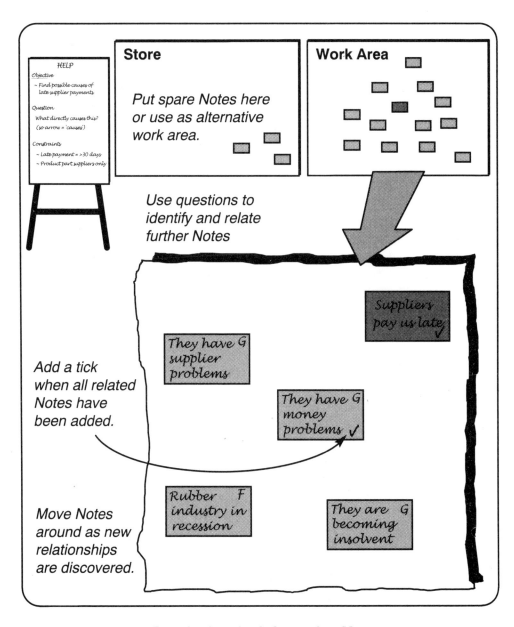

Developing the Information Map

6. Add arrows to show relationships

For each Note, ask the same questions from Step 5 to discover and position the Notes, this time adding arrows to show the relationship.

As each Note is completed, cross out the tick that was added in Step 5, enabling you to see which Notes have been processed.

Beware of adding too many arrows, which can result in the useful information in the map becoming obscured. This can happen when indirect relationships are shown as well as direct ones. For example, a broken vase is directly related to it hitting a wall, but is only indirectly related to the anger of the person throwing it.

If more Note chunks are discovered during this step, simply slip them in and add arrows as appropriate.

If you are drawing an arrow to a distant Note and the line crosses other lines, you can prevent any confusion by adding a 'hump' to jump over the crossed lines.

Although the arrows should all have the same meaning (such as 'causes'), you may sometimes find relationships that do not follow these rules but are still worth noting (such as 'has some kind of impact on'). In these cases, use a dotted arrow to show that it is does not have the same meaning as the other arrows. For example, in the diagram, the known recession in the rubber industry probably has an impact on a supplier's ability to pay, but is not considered to be a direct cause.

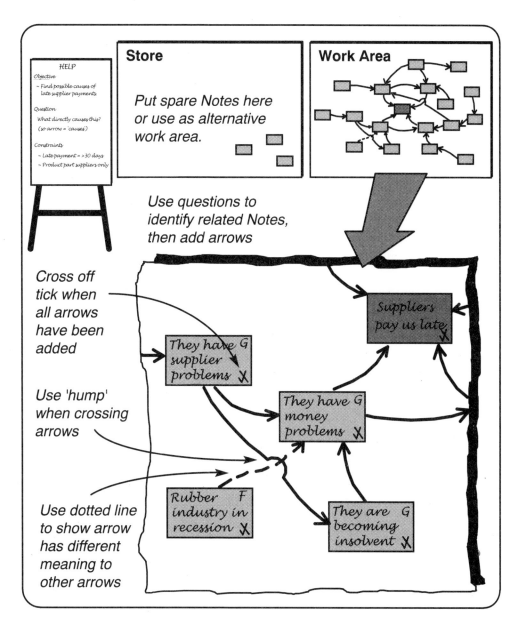

Adding arrows to the Information Map

7. Check completed map

When the Information Map is finished, check that all relationships are found and correctly shown with arrows.

If you are uncertain about the relationships or the completeness of the information in the map, it may be a good idea to leave it for an incubation period, coming back to it from time to time to see if you want to make any changes to it.

When you are happy that the map is complete, use it for its intended purpose, for example to identify key causes for further action.

Information Map Keys

- Define questions to help you identify Notes and relationships.
- Place one or more root problem Notes centrally.
- Identify related Notes by consistently asking a defined question.
- Put related Notes near one another.
- Add arrows to show relationships.

9 The Action Map

What is it for?

To show how a set of actions are related.

When do I use it?

An Action Map is concerned with *doing*. It answers questions such as, 'What must we do first?'. Use it when you are mapping any set of tasks or actions, to show how they depend on one another, for example, one task must be completed before another may start.

Use it to understand the logical sequence of tasks. By asking 'What *could* I do next?', you may find that after a particular task is completed, there are several more that could be done at the same time or in any chosen order.

Use it to plot the sequence of tasks, asking 'What *shall* I do next?' to make firm decisions on what to do when. It can be a good idea to find the logical sequence first, then rearrange the tasks into the actual sequence in which you will do them.

You can be use it to map out work processes, either as they exist or as you expect them to be performed. The map may then become a part of standards documentation.

It can also be of value when planning projects. Use a Top-down Tree to break up the problem into individual tasks, then use an Action Map to organize their sequence.

How does it work?

A common problem with any set of actions is to decide what must be done, and in what order. From the big picture of how a company operates down to production-line assembly, work processes need to be understood, designed, communicated and followed. The Action Map is a form of the more general Information Map and is specifically intended to solve this group of problems.

The Notes in an Action Map usually represent specific actions, which may range from broad functions such as, 'sell products' to more specific acts such as 'choose cereal' or 'insert screw'. The arrows usually indicate sequence, meaning 'is followed by'.

Most maps reflect a similar level of action in each Note. Thus you would not expect to find 'build rocket' and 'insert screw' on the same map. Multiple levels of action can be accommodated by *nesting*–a single Note on one map is expanded into an entire map at the next level down. In this fashion, the activities of an entire organization may be mapped.

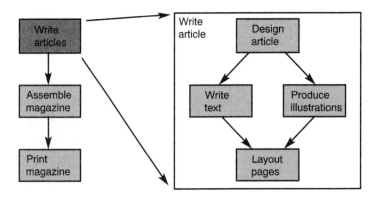

Nesting Action Maps

Action Maps often start at one point and finish at another. These points may be shown by Notes with 'Start' and 'End' written on them. Progress towards completion tends to be indicated by most arrows pointing in the general direction of the end point.

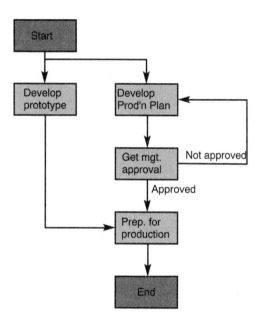

Action Map

How do I do it?

1. Identify objective

Identify your objective and set up the meeting as described in Chapter 3.

There are typically two levels of objective that are captured for Actions Maps: first, there are objectives relating to the use of the plan or process map, for example:

- Redesign key business processes to align with our stated market strategy.
- Reduce assembly time of XM30 engine.
- Bring new dress range to market.

The second level helps to give further direction when building the map, for example:

- Identify key business processes and how they interrelate.
- Map current assembly process of XM30 engine.
- Build plan for market promotion, showing tasks and how they depend on one another.

2. Identify constraints

Add constraints that must be considered, often those that focus around time, cost (including equipment and people) and quality. They may also indicate the level of detail required. For example:

- Must fit on a single page and be easily understood.
- Include each movement of part or person.
- It should be possible to allocate each task to one person and take less than 20hrs of effort.

Help

Guide-
lines for
session.

Store

*Use as storage for
Spare Notes and
as a spare work area.*

Work Area

*Put Notes here
during session to build
Action Map.*

HELP

<u>*Objectives*</u>

Overall:
   *~ Bring new rainwear range
     to market.*

Specific:
   *~ Identify tasks and dependencies
     for training sales force.*

<u>*Constraints*</u>

   *~ Plan must be implemented
     within the month of April.*
   ~ Must be done within budget.
   *~ Only 3 people in marketing dept
     available to implement it.*

Include high- and
low-level objectives

Objectives and constraints for Action Map

3. Identify expected map shape

Identify the expected shape from the type of map you are building and use it to help lay out the map. This will reduce the number of times Notes have to be reorganized to make more room. For example:

- Show a single person's process as a simple sequence of actions set out in the same order as they are performed. Use separate branches to show alternative sets of actions after a decision is made. These maps are often long and narrow, so start from the top of the Work Area and build the map downwards.
- When mapping a high-level process, use arrows to show the movement of items or information between sub-processes. This gives a broad diagram which may flow in several directions at once, and is best done either left to right or outwards from the middle (starting with the key processes).
- Build a plan by using arrows only to show what *must* follow what. This wide diagram is best laid out left to right.

Begin the map with a 'Start' Note to make it easier to read the flow from the beginning.

4. Map out what happens first

The initial action Notes simply ask 'What must happen first?' Place them to show that they follow the start and are independent of one another. Thus, when building the map from left to right, put them one above the other, spaced out sufficiently to enable later Notes to be added.

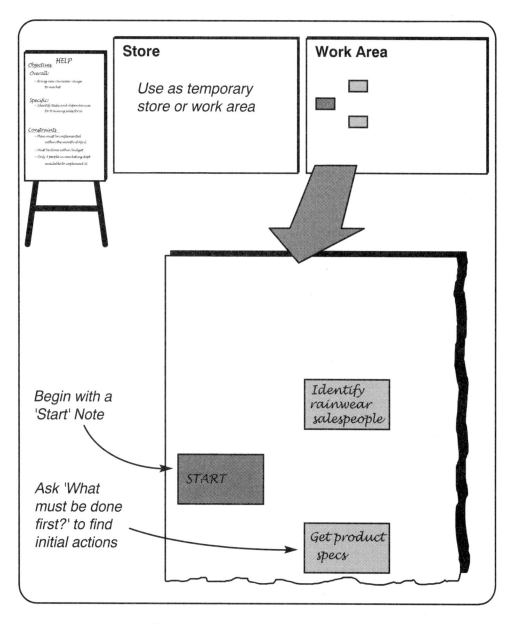

Starting to build the Action Map

5. Add subsequent actions

Continue to build the map by asking 'What immediately follows this?' of each Note added. Then write a Note, placing it so it is clear that it follows the previous action.

Quite often it will become apparent that an action should be done earlier or later. When this happens, simply rearrange the Notes to suit.

If a Note action follows more than one other Note, for example where the preceding actions produce items that are all used in this action, position the Note between the two and to the right of them both.

Some actions are not easily identified by asking 'What happens next?' In such cases there are a few alternative strategies:

- Do a Post-up first, to identify tasks for selection when building the map. This may involve quite a lot of moving around of Notes and combining those which are too detailed, but is useful for creative or uncertain situations.
- Use a Top-down Tree to break down the problem, then use the bottom level leaves as actions in the map. This is particularly useful for building plans.
- Start in the middle with well-known actions and work outwards, asking what must be done before and after each Note. Another variation is to start at the end and work backwards.

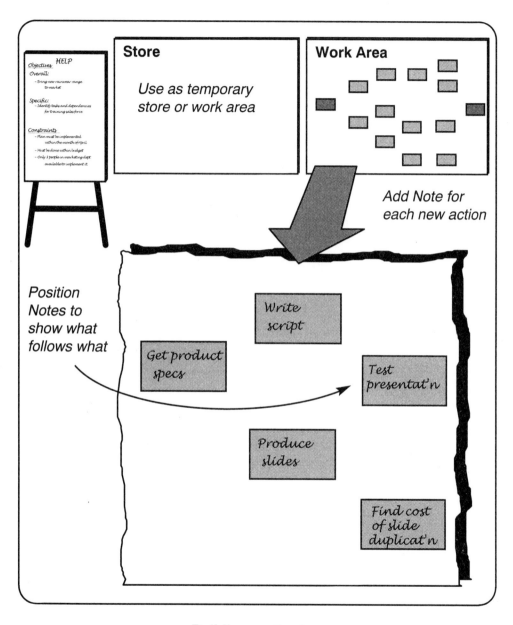

Building up the tree

6. Add arrows to show sequence

When the Map is complete, add an 'End' Note, positioning it just past the last Note. Start and end Notes help to contain the map, clearly showing it as one process or plan.

Go back through it again, adding arrows to show the sequence of actions. If arrows cross one another, use a 'hoop' to indicate that they do not join together.

Avoid adding arrows whilst generating Notes in earlier steps. Although it can be helpful to show unclear sequences, Notes often get moved when new actions or sequences are identified.

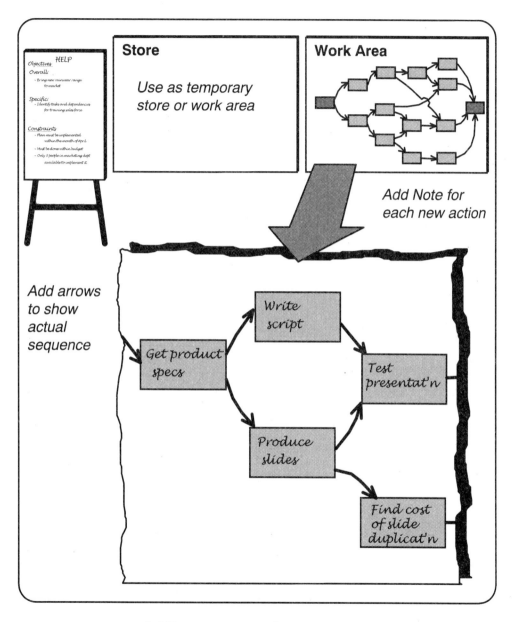

Adding arrows to show sequence

7. Check completed map

When the Action Map is complete, check that the objectives and constraints can be met.

It is not uncommon to produce several relatively small Action Maps, nested together as on page 90, rather than one large one. In this case, the next step may be to select one Note from the completed map and expand it to a new, lower level Action Map.

Action Map Keys

- Define objective and constraints.
- Find actions by asking 'What happens next?'
- Keep actions about the same size. Use nesting if appropriate.
- Position Notes in sequence order.
- Add arrows at end to show sequence.

Part III

Putting the Post-it® Note Tools to Work

The Post-it® Note Tools are for use in real problem-solving, and to make them work well requires an organized approach. When you are familiar with the tools and approaches to using them, you can then start innovating further, combining tools and devising new ways to use them.

Putting the Post-it® Note Tools to work

10 Solving problems

It was Rudyard Kipling who wrote the following lines which contain the passwords of problem-solvers everywhere:

> *I keep six honest serving men*
> *(They taught me all I knew);*
> *Their names are What and Why and When*
> *And How and Where and Who.*

The simplest way of taking Kipling's advice is to adopt a general questioning approach to problems. Thus, when faced with an uncertain situation, ask: 'What is important? Why should it be fixed? Where are the facts?' and so on. It is amazing how much you can achieve just by being open-minded and not accepting the status quo.

The questioning approach, although useful, can still leave you unsure about where to start and what to do next. Asking questions may help, but it may also confuse if they are the wrong questions for the current place, time and person.

A good solution is to organize yourself in such a way that you approach a problem with a reasonable degree of confidence. One way is to use a rigid set of rules that prescribe every step. This may work on a few types of problem, but can be too inflexible in many other situations.

An alternative is to use more flexible guidelines that may be adapted to fit the problem in hand. This *framework* provides the bones of the problem-solving method, but allows you to define the more detailed actions within each stage.

Generally, the size and complexity of the framework will reflect the size and importance of the problem. It makes sense to spend time and effort in solving serious and costly problems, but smaller, everyday problems need a more lightweight approach.

There are three frameworks you can use:

1. For everyday problems, take a general *questioning approach* and use the Post-it® Note tool that seems most applicable.

2. For more challenging problems, use the *simple framework* as described on the page opposite. Use Post-it® Note tools individually or in combination to help solve the problem.

3. For serious problems that require more organization, assemble a team of people who can work together to solve the problem and use the *project framework* as described.

A simple framework

When faced with any problem, begin by using these few basic steps:

1. *What are you trying to achieve?* If you can describe where you are trying to get to, then you are more likely to be able to get there.

2. *What is the <u>real</u> problem?* Select the best tool to organize and understand the information around the problem. Use a Post-up to gather information. Organize it with a Tree for simple situations and Map for more complicated ones. Look for the important things to fix. If they are not clear, use a Swap Sort.

3. *What is the solution?* <u>Use</u> the results to obtain a better understanding of the problem and then find an appropriate solution. Do a Post-up to find possible solutions and a Swap Sort to find the best one.

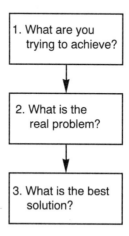

A simple framework

A Project Framework

Difficult and important problems merit a more formal approach to those problems addressed by questioning or the simple framework.

The framework described here is built on just three of Kipling's questions: What? Why? and How? Within the framework, of course, many more questions may be asked.

A feature of the framework is that it takes steps to find the *cause* of the problem before trying to find a suitable solution. This approach ensures that you treat the real problem, and not just the symptoms.

The framework also seeks not only to fix the problem, but to ensure that it stays fixed and that you learn from the experience so that future problems become easier to solve.

The main steps are as follows:

1. **What** is the problem?
2. **Why** is it happening?
3. **How** can you fix it?
4. *– Fix it! –*
5. **Why** did it work or not work?
6. **What** next?

The following sections expand on each of these steps, and suggest which tools may be used.

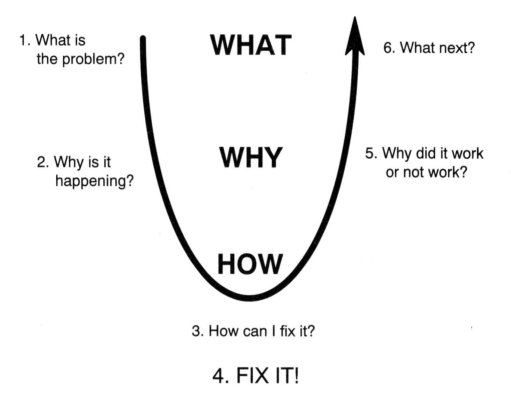

1. What is
   the problem?

WHAT

6. What next?

2. Why is it
   happening?

WHY

5. Why did it work
   or not work?

HOW

3. How can I fix it?

4. FIX IT!

The project framework

1. What is the problem?

Defining the problem is often a messy stage. You know you are hurting, but do not really know what is wrong. The first task is to create problem and goal statements to help you focus your efforts. They will also help you later to tell whether the problem has been fixed.

Spend some time on this stage, as it can require a fair amount of effort to gather the facts about a problem. If you are in a hurry, you may want to skip through it more quickly, but be prepared to recognize this in Step 5 (Why did it work or not work?).

Why are we here?

To set the context of the project, create a brief *problem statement*, outlining the basic problem and why you need to fix it now.

Where possible, include facts and figures and indicate why this problem is more urgent than others. For example, 'Deliveries have been consistently late over the past six months, resulting in about 50 complaints from major customers. Several customers are threatening to move to the competition.' This statement paints the 'big picture' which gives urgency and direction to all future actions.

- Use a Post-up to help gather information on the problem.
- Organize the results of the Post-up in a Bottom-up Tree to help find the problem statement.
- Alternatively use an Information Map to connect the results of the Post-up.

What are we trying to achieve?

Create a *goal statement*, or ultimate objective, which describes what the situation will look like when you have solved the immediate problem.

You can have multiple goal statements, but they may complicate the solution as you try to solve all things at once. In fact it is usually safer to fix things one piece at a time, as big changes require big efforts and can fail in many different ways.

Aim to base your goal on facts, rather than opinions. Take time to measure things like current customer complaint levels, along with other factors such as how severe the complaints are.

A good goal statement helps you identify when the problem is fixed and implies some kind of continuing measurement. For example, 'Within the next half-year, reduce customer complaints about Keydo products to less than three per month.'

- Draw an Action Map of the process being fixed, to clarify what happens and identify measurement points.
- Use a Swap Sort to choose the best measurement.
- Do a Post-up of possible goals. Use the problem statement and Action Map already generated to help focus this effort, for example by spotting problem areas to be measured. To decrease defects by 50 per cent means that you have to know what they are now!
- Use a Swap Sort to choose the best goal.
- Do an Action Map to plan the rest of the project, including people needed and tasks to be completed.

2. Why is it happening?

When you know what your problem is, the next step is to find out why it is happening.

Have you ever tried answering a small child who keeps asking you 'But *why?*'. By about the fifth 'why', if you are still there, you are likely to have reached quite a detailed level. The Japanese recognize this and have a saying: 'Ask why five times.'

Beware of skipping this stage. It is a common trap to leap from problem to solution without considering whether you are fixing the cause or just treating symptoms.

- Do a Top-down Tree (asking Why?) to find out what is causing the problem.
- Alternatively, use an Information Map to map complex cause relationships.
- Use a Swap Sort to determine the most important causes to fix. As with goals, keep the number of causes to fix at one time down to a manageable and practical number.

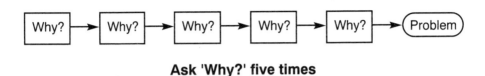

Ask 'Why?' five times

3. How can I fix it?

When you have defined your problem and identified causes, the next step is to apply the same technique of finding a number of alternative solutions and narrowing them down to a few that you are going to implement.

When selecting solutions, make sure that you are able to fully implement them. The simplest way is to find actions for which you do not need authorization and where you do not have to persuade other people to implement the solution.

Beware of finding fault with other people–the result is likely to be conflict and nothing implemented.

If other people are affected by your solution, then take time to organize your information and be prepared to negotiate and persuade. They might have to give you permission or resources to enable you to implement your solution, or you may want them to do something for you–possibly even permanently change what they do.

- Do a Post-up of potential solutions.
- Alternatively, use a Top-down Tree, starting with the cause from Step 2 and asking 'How?' in order to find the detail of how the problem may be fixed.
- Use a Swap Sort to select the best solution.

4. Fix it!

This stage is where you implement the solution identified in Step 3.

Although it may seem simple to put into effect the solution that you are sure will fix the problem, many projects stumble at this stage, where theories are turned into practices and commitments must turn into actions.

If other people are involved in implementing the solution, make sure they receive adequate training. What they should do may be clear to you, but it must be crystal clear to them.

It can also be tempting at this stage to make last-minute changes, using different solutions that suddenly seem better. If you are tempted down this path be prepared to face the consequences in Step 5–if the wonderful new fix does not work, you will be asked embarrassing questions as to why.

- Do an Action Map of the steps to take in implementing the solution. Include actions to ensure people understand any changes that affect them. Also plan to measure the changes in some way so you can tell whether the solution has worked.

5. Why did it work or not work?

After implementing the solution to the problem, stand back and watch. With luck, it will work as planned, but the best laid plans do not always work as expected. It is thus important to treat the solution as being 'on trial' until it has proved itself.

If the solution did not work as planned, you should look at how the process failed, *not* apportion blame to people.

The most important part of this stage is to *learn* about both the problem in hand and the overall problem-solving process. Write these lessons down so that you clarify your own thoughts and can pass this learning (not blaming!) on to others.

- Do a Post-up and Bottom-up Tree to identify reasons for success or failure. Ask: Why did it happen as it did? What were the key reasons?
- Do an Action Map of actual events, then compare this with the plan from Step 3. Ask: What unexpected events occurred? What was not planned? What unnecessary actions were planned?

6. What next?

What you do next depends very much on what went before. There are three possible actions you can take:

1. *If the solution did not work*, go back to a previous step to find a solution that will work. For example, if Step 5 showed that the identified cause from Step 2 was not that critical after all, then go back to Step 2 and find a real cause to fix. Where a solution did not work because in practice it proved to be unworkable, go back to Step 3.

2. *If the solution did work*, go back to a previous step to make further improvements–either to Step 2 to fix another identified cause, or to Step 1, to find a new problem to fix or to refine the goal in order to fix a new part of the problem.

3. Whether the solution worked or not, close down the project. The problem should now be fixed or perhaps it turned out to be not worth the effort to solve. The subsequent action may be to celebrate, to disband or to start another project.

- Do a Swap Sort of possible subsequent actions.
- Do an Action Map to plan the next steps.

11 Post-it® Note Tools in Action

Now that Post-it® Note tools have been explained in detail and suggestions given for how they may be used in structured problem-solving situations, this chapter presents a more complete example of how they may be used in practice.

The episode described here involves a number of the Note tools, showing how they can be used to help solve actual problems.

The problem

Peter Rogers, the Technology Services manager, stared worriedly at the piece of paper. The memo from Jane Hughes, the Operations Manager, was typical of a steady stream of complaints that he had been receiving about his department and the services that they provided to the company. He sighed, put the paper down and rubbed his forehead, wondering what to do next.

By the next departmental meeting Peter had decided what action to take, and as he described the problem and his proposals to his people, he was gratified to see that they took the situation seriously. When they started discussing it, however, it became clear that there was much disagreement as to the true nature of the problem and, by the coffee break, no progress had been made.

Step 1: What is the problem?

As they sipped their coffee, Peter stood up and explained what they must do. It was the team's problem and they must work together to solve it. They would use a project framework to find the problem and make sure it was properly fixed. Within this framework, they would use Notes to capture and understand the pieces of the problem.

The first step was to discover the fundamental problem. To help collect their thoughts, Peter decided to use a Post-up. This would start in the meeting and then would be left up for a week, so people could add facts, opinions and ideas as they came to light.

In the meeting they identified twenty-five Note thoughts. Another ten were added during the week. The Help page and final Post-Up are shown below.

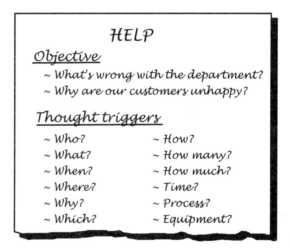

Help page for Post-Up to find problem

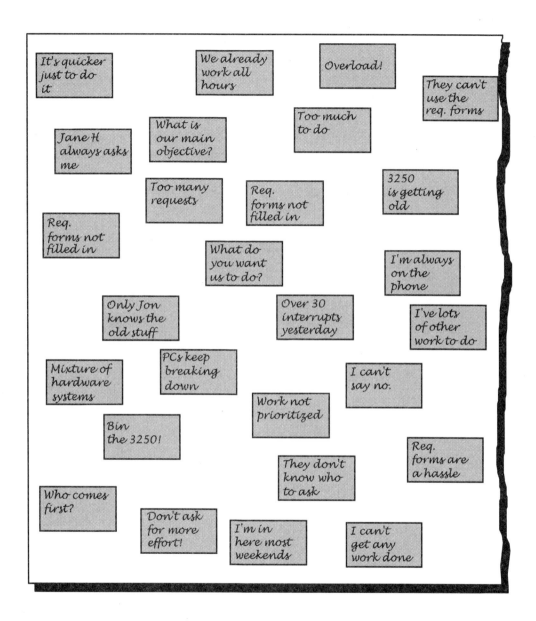

Posting up information chunks on the problem

At the end of the week, they sat and looked at the problem. After a period of silence, Geraint Morgan, a junior analyst, pointed out what everyone else was already thinking: that he still did not understand the basic problem. Sure, there were many valid points there, but what did they add up to?

Peter nodded slowly as others murmured their agreement.

'You're right, Geraint', he said, as he taped a couple of pieces of flipchart paper together to make a new work area, 'And I think a Bottom-up Tree will help us make sense of this. The help page can stay the same, but there are a few new rules for you to learn ...'

Before long, the only sound was the flutter of paper and scratching of heads as they gradually moved the Notes into columns of related issues. Silent battles raged as individuals moved Notes back and forth between columns, but at last a peace was found as people either agreed or made duplicates. Some new Notes were also added as the structure of the problem gradually dawned.

Adding header Notes was surprisingly easy as everyone soon agreed on the meaning of each column. This final agreement also allowed the last few 'orphan' Notes to find a home in one of the existing columns.

Peter added a couple of Notes above the headers and linked them to the headers with lines to show where problems were felt internally or externally to the department.

As a summary, they agreed on a problem statement as follows:

We are working hard, trying to keep up with requests from our customers, but have become so interrupt-driven that we have lost sight of what we are trying to achieve.

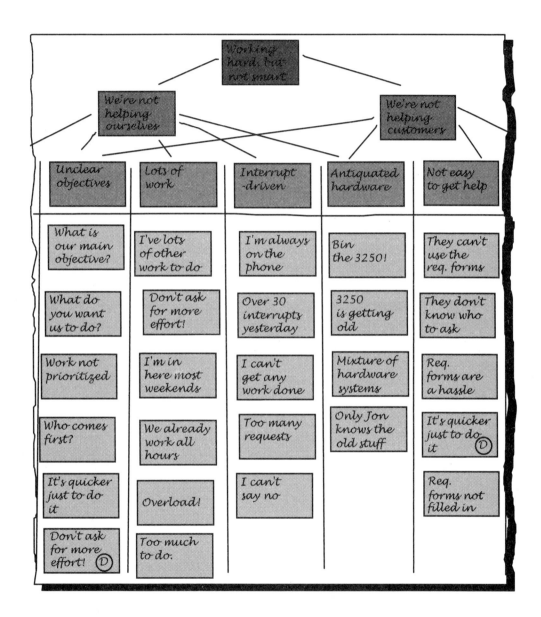

Bottom-up Tree to find basic problem

Now that the main problems were identified, several people had ideas for fixing them and were all for implementing their solutions straight away.

'Hold on, folks!' called Peter, smiling at the enthusiasm. 'We want to be sure that we are fixing the right thing before we rush into action. Let's use a Swap Sort to help.'

When writing the Help page, there was some discussion over the priority of different criteria, but Peter was very clear that customer problems were more important than their internal, departmental problems.

Using the criteria, the problems from the Bottom-up Tree were easily sorted into order of importance.

From this, they created a goal statement:

Our customers can get help in a way that helps us to help them, resulting in their increased satisfaction with our service to them.

HELP

Objective

~ Which problem should we tackle first?

Criteria

1. Increases customer satisfaction
2. Makes life easier for us
3. Is within our current capability

Help page for Swap Sort to find key problem to fix

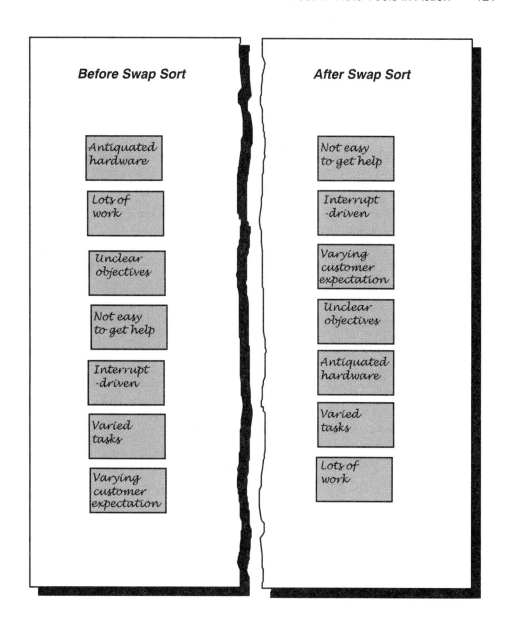

Swap Sort to find key problem to fix

Step 2: Why is it happening?

'Ok' said Peter, looking around at his team. 'We now know where we stand and where we want to get to. The next step is to find out why it is happening.'

There were immediately a number of suggestions, most of which were ideas to fix the problem, rather than its causes. Thankful for the structure that the project framework gave, Peter hauled them back and explained what they would do next.

They decided to tackle the top two problems, as this allowed them to consider both the external, customer concern and the internal, departmental problems. As these two problems seemed to be inextricably connected, Peter decided to use an Information Map to understand this relationship and find the key causes.

HELP

Objective

~ *Why is it not easy for our customers to get help?*
~ *Why are we so interrupt-driven?*

Question

What directly causes this?
(so arrow = 'causes')

Help page for Information Map to find problem causes

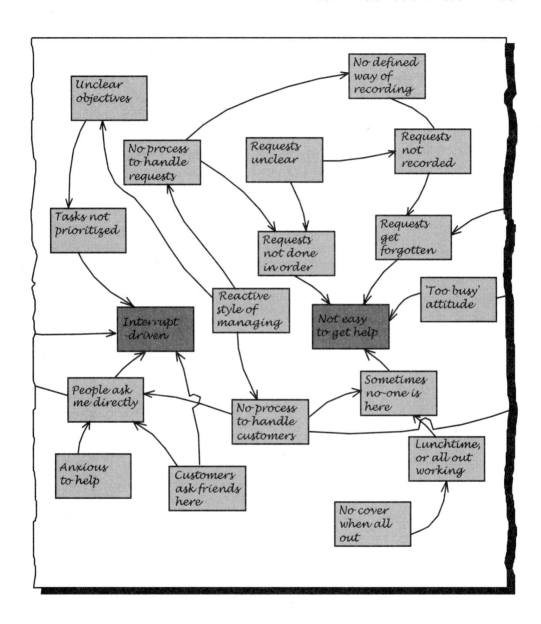

Information Map to find problem causes

Step 3: How can we fix it?

'Of course!'

They all agreed that the Information Map made the causes of their problem much clearer. Their focus had been on running the main systems and they had not recognized that requests for help was also an important process.

The next step was to find a solution. The Information Map made it clear that there was a pressing need for a process to handle customer requests.

'Before building the process description, I think a Top-down Tree would help us to identify the tasks that must be completed.' Peter was becoming confident in the power of the Post-it® Note tools to help them work together to rapidly solve each part of the problem.

HELP

<u>Objective</u>
~ Find tasks in the request
   handling process

<u>Questions</u>
Identify (find children of parents):
~ What tasks will have
   to be done?

Check (for complete family):
~ Do all children, taken together,
   make up the parent?

Help page for Top-down Tree of tasks

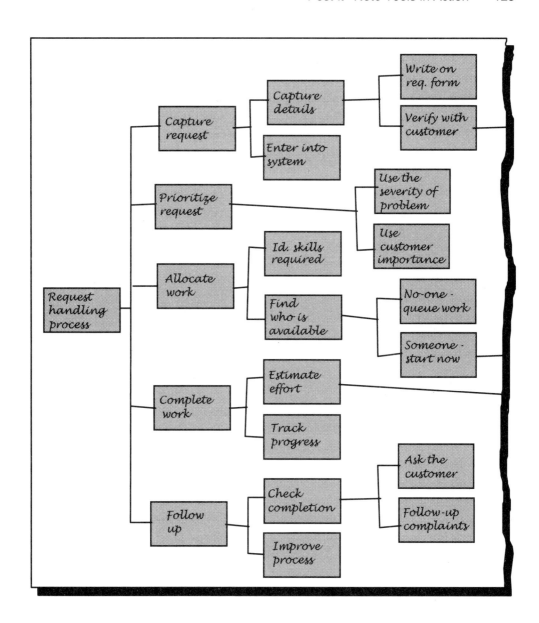

Top-down Tree of tasks

As a technology group, they were familiar with process charting techniques and several of them were keen to use a fairly detailed method of designing the request handling process. Peter, however, pulled these back, pointing out how an Action Map was just as good, and would be a much quicker way of piecing together the steps of the process.

Once they started mapping the process, even the doubters became enthusiastic, as the solution rapidly took shape.

They later used a copy of the map of the final process to help persuade and train other people affected by the process, including their end customers.

HELP

Objective

~ *Overall : To efficiently and effectively satisfy customers' needs for help.*

~ *Specifically : To define process to handle customer requests.*

Constraints

~ *No extra people available.*

~ *Some of existing budget may be available.*

Help page for Action Map of request handling process

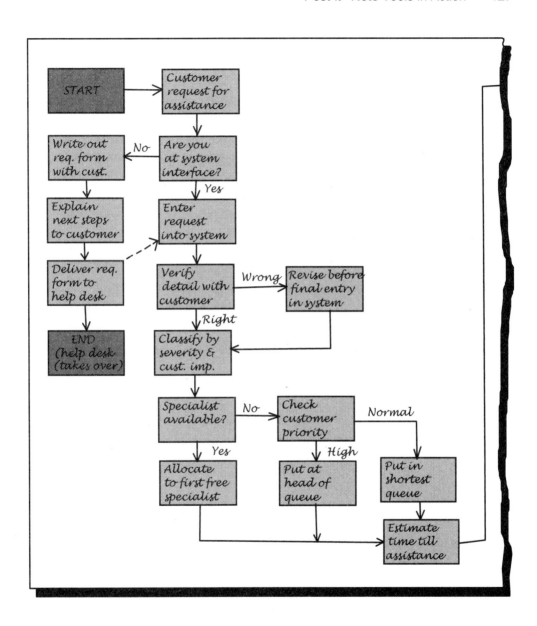

Action Map of request handling process

Step 4: Fix it!

'That was surprisingly quick!' remarked Heledd De Lune, the response team leader. 'From confused to action in just over a week. It must be a record!'

Peter smiled. 'There's one last thing to do before we put it into action, and that's to confirm who's doing what. The Action Map has helped, but I want to be sure that all the responsibilities are understood.'

He then drew some columns on the whiteboard and took out the Notes. Several people smiled. They knew that this would be another quick and effective session.

Peter explained that he wanted to check that all of the high-level tasks were owned. He was now comfortable enough with the main Post-it® Note tools to try his own variation, based on the Post-up.

> ## HELP
>
> ### Objective
> ~ Allocate responsibility for key tasks.
>
> ### Constraints
> ~ Use current skills and positions.

Help page for modified Post-up to check responsibilities

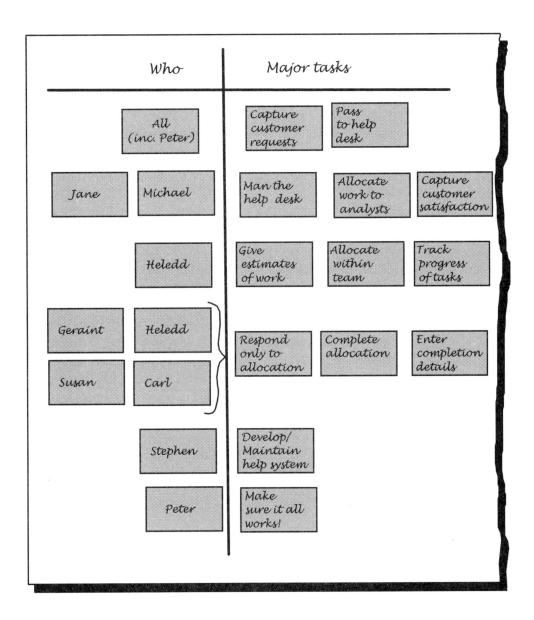

Modified Post-up to allocate responsibilities

Step 5: Why did it work or not work?

At the end of the first month of operation, they all sat down together to discuss how well the process was working in the 'real world'.

For the most part it had been very successful, with some glowing feedback on the improvements. In particular, several financial analysts had praised their responsiveness to a couple of problems in the salary administration system.

They were, however, disappointed to have received some rather irate feedback from the development manager. He had put in a high-priority request for assistance with machine configuration, but had not received any help for three days.

'Why did this happen?' asked Peter.

'Well, I've checked that the request was put into the system on Monday.' said Michael.

'But I didn't get it until Thursday,' said Susan.

'Then why did it get stuck in the process?' asked Peter.

'Let's use the Notes to model what actually happened.' suggested Heledd. 'If we make one Note represent one request, we can watch the queue to see what happened.'

Peter readily agreed to this, pleased that suggestions for using the Notes were now coming from the team, and a short time later, the evidence was plain–the finance problems had also come in as high priority and had been put ahead of the development manager's problems. As both problems were for Susan, she did not receive the development manager's problems until both finance problems were completed.

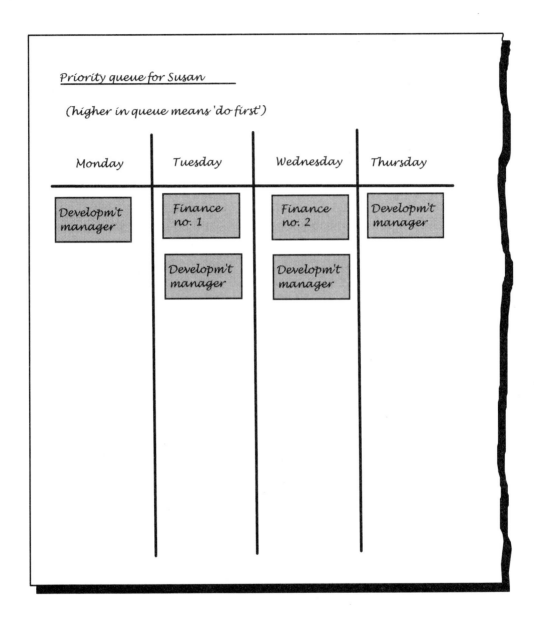

Using Notes to model the request queue

Step 6: What next?

The next step was now clear. The process needed correction to prevent some high priority requests being pushed down the list by other high priority requests. The solution was found by adjusting the Action Map and the corresponding system controls.

They then went back to Step 4 to check the system again, following through each step carefully, ensuring that the changed process worked as planned, and that any discovered problems were recognized and their cause found and eliminated.

In the following months, a few more problems were found, their causes determined and appropriate changes made to the process to cope with them. Post-it® Notes continued to be useful tools for finding the problems, and all six tools were used at one time or another.

In the review meeting six months after they had started, Peter showed them a graph of the customer satisfaction index that they had been measuring. It showed how satisfaction had risen and was now steady at an all-time high.

In drawing the project to a close, they concluded that the framework and tools had provided just the right amount of guidance without being too restrictive. In the later states, their increasing familiarity with the principles of the Post-it® Note tools had allowed them to use variations of the basic tools, shaping their use to the specific need of each step.

12 Advanced Usage

When you have been using the tools for a while and are comfortable with how they work, you could continue using them as described in the previous chapters or in whatever form you have found that works well for you.

On the other hand, you could adopt a deliberate strategy of steadily pushing back the boundaries and looking for new ways of making better and more effective use of Post-it® Notes in your own problem solving.

This chapter looks further at some of the other ways that Notes can be used, including:

- Extending or changing the rules for existing tools to make them easier to use or to solve a specific problem.
- Combining existing tools so they work in harmony to solve a single problem.
- Inventing completely new tools to use in your particular work environment.

The examples given here can be used as described or can act as inspiration for you to find your own way of advancing the use of Post-it® Notes in rapid problem-solving.

Extending the standard tools

To extend the standard tools, first examine and gain a good understanding of both the basic rules and the situation where you want a better way of solving the problem. The next step is to change the rules and try it out.

Accelerated Swap Sort

In the standard rules for the Swap Sort, the Notes are initially randomly placed in a vertical list. You can speed the sort by putting the Notes that you think are more important nearer the top of the list. If you are correct, this will result in less swaps, which is particularly useful if you have a longer list.

A second way of accelerating the Swap Sort is to compare and swap *any* pair of Notes. Thus, if a Note at the bottom of the list looks important, you can compare and swap it with the top Note.

Nothing is free, and the price you pay in both of these variations is that as you make less comparisons you reduce the chance of making breakthrough discoveries where a Note that was initially considered unimportant is discovered to be more valuable.

1. Start with list in
   approximate order
   of priority.

2. Swap any pair
   of notes.

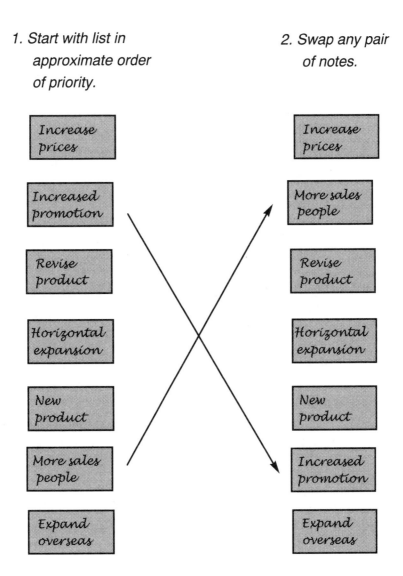

Accelerated Swap Sort

The Inside-out Tree

You can start a Top-down Tree in the middle and work both ways. If you go down the tree by asking 'How?' you go up even further by asking 'Why?'. You can then find alternative solutions by going back down a different branch.

For example, if a person asks for promotion, ask 'Why?' to find it is for recognition, then 'How?' to discover a high visibility project that is an equally acceptable alternative.

Investigation Top-down Tree

When using a Top-down Tree, you can vary the question asked at each level, going from the original problem down to the solution and risk management in a single tree, as shown in the example opposite.

A problem when using Top-down Trees like this to go down a number of levels is that at the lower levels you start running out of space in the Work Area.

If you are able to focus on specific Notes as you build the tree, you can control the space problem by using the principles of divergence and convergence to develop only those branches that are of specific interest or look more promising than the others.

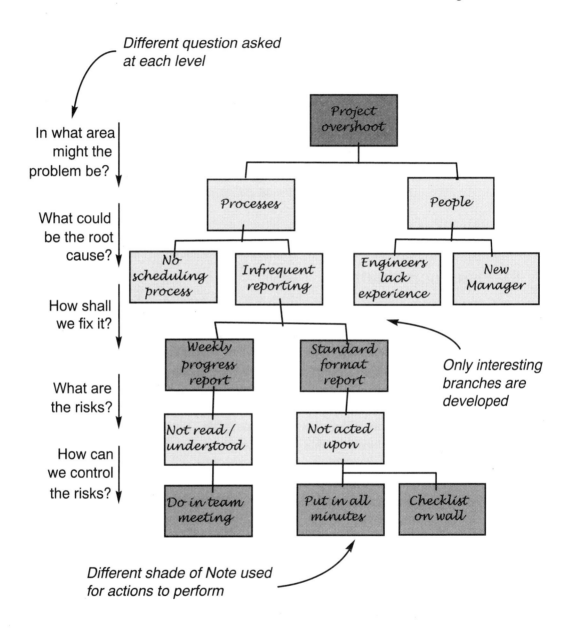

Investigation Top-down Tree

Combining tools

Tools are useful when used alone, but can be particularly powerful when used in combination, especially when the Notes from using one tool are simply transferred across to use on another tool.

The simplest and most common form of combining tools is when the results of a Post-up are used as an input to other tools. This principle can be extended for specific situations, as in the following examples.

Planning combinations

Post-it® Notes are ideal for planning, as this is an activity that is often confusing. Grand high-level plans degenerate into chaos as you try to turn strategies into actionable tactics.

The illustration shows how a high-level objective can be broken down in a Top-down Tree. The bottom-level leaves should be actionable tasks which will usually be allocated to individuals and will be trackable (hint: if you track activity on a weekly basis, then most tasks should take about one week).

These bottom-level leaves can now be moved directly into an Action Map. As well as saving time, this method ensures that all actions are carried forward.

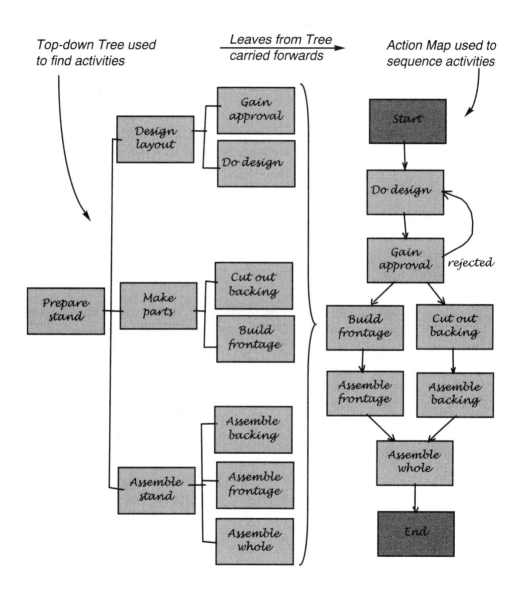

Planning combinations

The Sorted Tree

When doing either a Top-down Tree or (especially) a Bottom-up Tree, you can end up with large families of Notes at the bottom of the Tree. Although the families are large, all members are not necessarily equal, for example where they are potential solutions to a problem.

This situation can be addressed by using a Swap Sort, sorting the families of leaves on the tree in situ, without having to move them away from their parent.

The Naked Tree

Trees appear naked in winter as they lose all of their leaves. This idea can be translated into a way of combining the Top-down Tree and the Post-up to structure creative sessions, giving them sufficient direction to enable faster resolution of your problems.

As shown in the illustration, you first do a Top-down Tree of the whole problem, breaking it down into the various subject areas in which you can be creative. Follow this with a short Post-up for each of the identified subject areas, putting the Notes in a column underneath the appropriate leaf of the Tree.

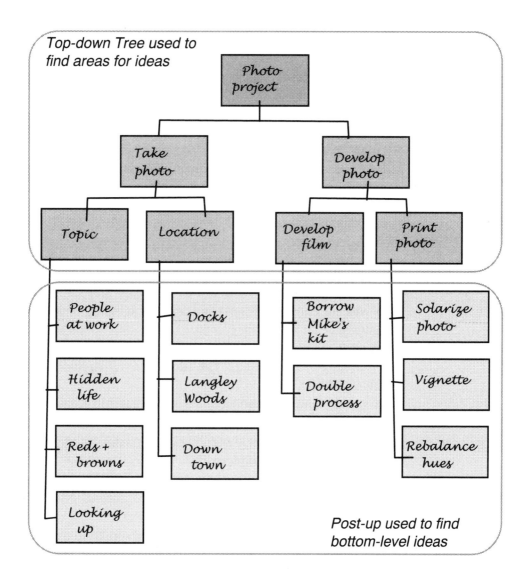

Top-down Tree used to find areas for ideas

Post-up used to find bottom-level ideas

Naked Tree: combining Top-down Tree and Post-up

Developing new tools

The principles of capturing chunks of information on Notes and organizing them can be used to develop completely new tools. As you become more practised and comfortable with using and extending the standard tools, you start thinking in a Post-it® Note kind of way which leads to the discovery of a host of new tools to solve individual problems.

Task timescales

The use of Notes during planning can be extended from the Top-down Tree and Action Map into a diagram showing who will be carrying out what action, and when it will be completed.

As with any development, borrow ideas from existing tools wherever appropriate. The illustration is derived from the classic Gantt Chart.

Columns show your reporting period, typically weeks or months, whilst rows show the people who will be working on the tasks. The tasks are placed as milestones, in the week where they are to be completed.

A further development of this diagram could be to show the duration of tasks, for example with a second Note per task showing the start point. Other variables associated with planning can also be added, such as the effort involved, the calendar time, the critical path, the free float, and so on.

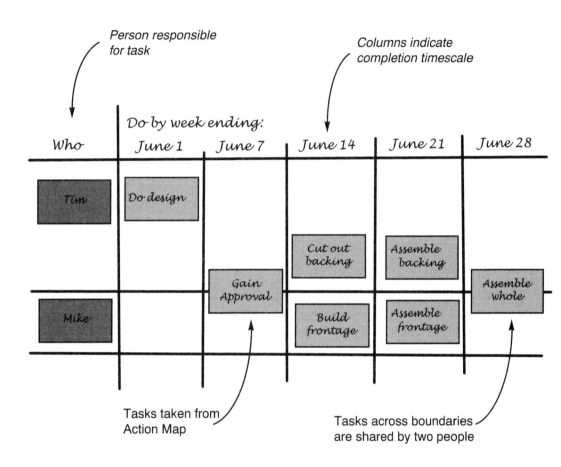

Person responsible
for task

Columns indicate
completion timescale

Do by week ending:

Who	June 1	June 7	June 14	June 21	June 28
Tim	Do design		Cut out backing	Assemble backing	
		Gain Approval			Assemble whole
Mike			Build frontage	Assemble frontage	

Tasks taken from
Action Map

Tasks across boundaries
are shared by two people

Developing new tool: Task timescales

Bottom-up Sets

In some problems, the relationships between various chunks are complex enough to indicate that an Information Map is required, but not sufficiently certain to be able to add arrows between Notes.

The required tool for this type of situation is somewhere between the grouping of the Bottom-up Tree and the complex structuring of the Information Map.

The answer is simply not to add arrows, but to move the Notes (after or during a Post-up) into overlapping groups of related chunks.

When you have done this, and if the boundary between groups is clear, you can draw circles around them forming overlapping sets.

A set, by the way, is another name for a non-ordered list. They become interesting, as indicated, when they overlap with one another.

Top-down Sets

Sets, like trees, can be built top-down as well as bottom-up. When you know what the groupings are going to be, define the sets first, drawing and naming overlapping circles, then use a Post-up to fill in the sets and overlaps, as in the illustration.

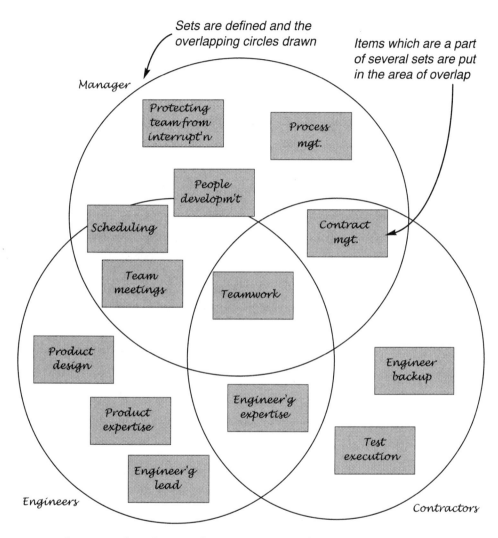

Sets are defined and the overlapping circles drawn

Items which are a part of several sets are put in the area of overlap

Manager

Protecting team from interrupt'n

Process mgt.

People developm't

Scheduling

Contract mgt.

Team meetings

Teamwork

Product design

Engineer backup

Product expertise

Engineer'g expertise

Test execution

Engineer'g lead

Engineers

Contractors

Objective: Identify Contribution to success of team members

Top-down Set

Advanced Usage?

Appendix: Practical Tips

Whenever you use tools of any sort, there are invariably certain tricks of the trade that help make the job quicker and easier and perform tasks that would otherwise seem almost impossible. Professionals tend to acquire these skills through a combination of sitting at the feet of their teachers and their own long experience.

This appendix does not aim to make you an instant maestro, but it may ease some of the difficulties experienced early on by adding a few helpful pointers.

On first using the tools...

The first time you use the tools, expect to be hesitant and uncertain. Expect that it will feel a bit awkward. But also recognize that you are in a learning situation, so also expect to improve with practice. Let your problems become interesting opportunities to find out how the tools work.

A good way of learning is in collaboration with other people, as the sharing of experience will help you all to grasp the practical principles of each tool more quickly than working alone. The tools described in this book work particularly well when used with a group, although you can also use them when working alone.

On peeling Post-it® Notes...

Post-it® Notes come in pads of around 100 Notes. When you peel them off backwards, the top part of the Note, where the adhesive is on the back curls. When you post them up on the wall, they tend to stick out at an awkward angle, rather than lying flat. They also have the tendency to fall off, especially if you are moving them around and have not pressed hard to make them stick well.

A simple solution is to pull the Notes off *diagonally forwards and slightly up*, not backwards, as in the illustration opposite. This may seem awkward at first, but once mastered gives a flatter, more usable Note.

Another solution is to buy packs of Pop-up® Notes (USA) or 'Z' Notes (Europe), which are deliberately stuck together in alternate directions to solve just this curly problem. These are best used in the special holders available for them. The Notes then can be very easily pulled out one at a time, much like tissues from a box.

Pop-up® Notes

Wrong: Note curls, then will not stick well
(ripped off backwards)

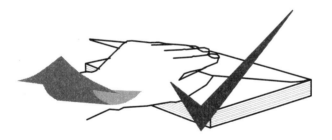

Right: Pulls off Note with minimum curl
(diagonally forwards and slightly up, towards you)

Pulling off Post-it® Note for minimum curl

On different sized Notes...

Post-it® Notes come in several different sizes, two of which are most useful in problem-solving.

The most popular size, three inches by five inches, is useful for working in groups, where Notes are stuck to a vertical surface, so that everyone can see them from a distance. To make them more readable, use a broad-pointed marker pen.

Smaller sized Notes, one-and-a-half inches by two inches, are useful when you are working alone or in a very small group. In this case, you can write on the Note in ordinary handwriting with a pen or pencil.

On different shades of Note...

As has been discussed in previous chapters, you can use more than the standard yellow Post-it® Notes. Use red, blue and yellow for the FOG factors (Facts, Opinions, Guesses) when doing Post-ups. Use red, blue and green for successive levels of header Notes in the Bottom-up Tree. Use a red root Note in the Information Map.

These are not the only places where you can use different shades of Note. For example, when changing the question in the Top-down Tree, also change the shade of the Note.

If you do not have a red or blue Note to hand, you can achieve a similar effect by using different shades of pen or by marking the Notes in some way, for example with broad borders.

This can be read from across the room.

Use large Notes for groups, with large writing so you can read it from a distance when it is stuck onto a wall.

This can be read only when you are close to it.

Use small Notes when working by yourself, or in very small groups, so you can fit more on the desktop.

Use the right size of Post-it® Note

On working surfaces...

Notes do not stick to every surface. They work best on a dry, smooth surface, such as a whiteboard or window. Perhaps the best surface is paper (after all, their original use was as a bookmark). They do not work on rough or dirty surfaces. If in doubt, test them by sticking a Note to the surface and blowing hard to see if you can dislodge it.

Whiteboards are useful for working with tools such as the Top-down Tree or either of the Maps, where you will probably want to draw and redraw lines between the Notes. The problem here, as with other large flat surfaces like walls and windows, is that you cannot take them away. If you wish to take a copy of your final diagram with you, you will have to transcribe it to a more transportable piece of paper.

Flipcharts enable you to take away or move around a group of Notes, but may be too small to contain a complete diagram. Compromise by taping several flipchart pages together to make a larger working area. You may alternatively use a large sheet of brown paper. Completed diagrams can then be transferred to the walls in your work room.

When working with small Notes, one-and-a-half inches by two inches, use a blank page in your workbook. You can then leave them there to reference or build the diagram gradually, as you walk around from place to place.

3M make a couple of additional products that can be used for working surfaces.

Post-it® Meeting Charts are a cross between Flipcharts and Post-it® Notes, having a broad strip of the special glue on the reverse across the top. This lets you quickly and easily stick them to walls without having to resort to tape or pins.

Post-it® Easel Roll is similar, but comes on a roll and has the adhesive on two edges, allowing a wide Store or Work Area to be firmly stuck to the wall.

On making the tools work for you...

When you first use the Post-up or Action Map or any of the other tools, it is a good idea to follow the guidelines given in this book, as they give a consistent approach that is easy to learn, use and share.

But if you find that the tools described here do not suit your way of working, do not be a slave to them. Once you are comfortable that you understand the practical principles, feel free to bend and change the rules to suit your way of working, like the examples in Chapter 12. Invent new uses or combine tools for new situations. You can even use the tools themselves for this task!

When changing the way you use the tools, do involve the people with whom you will be using them. If they are changed to suit just you, then you will lose the great benefits to be gained by using them in groups.